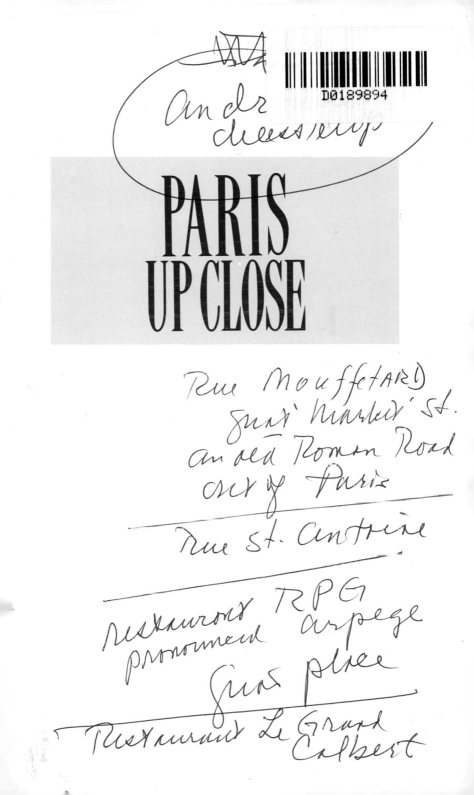

Andr
chessieuji

PARIS
UP CLOSE

Rue Mouffetard
great market St.
an old Roman Road
out of Paris

Rue St. Antoine

Restaurant RPG
pronounced Arpege
great place

Restaurant Le Grand
Colbert

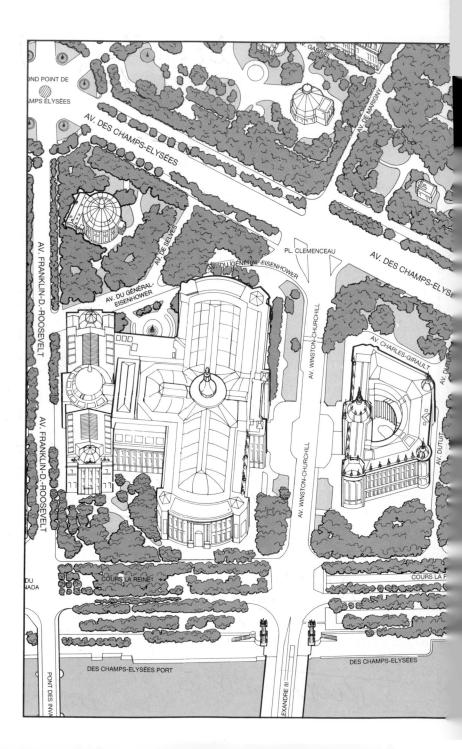

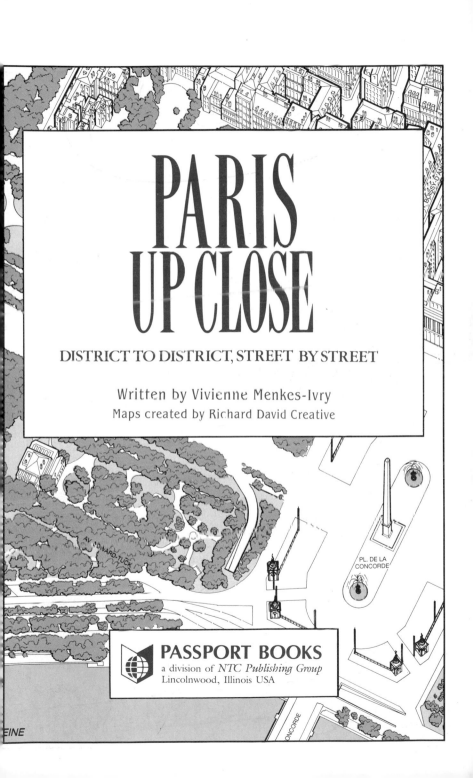

PARIS
UP CLOSE

DISTRICT TO DISTRICT, STREET BY STREET

Written by Vivienne Menkes-Ivry

Maps created by Richard David Creative

PASSPORT BOOKS
a division of *NTC Publishing Group*
Lincolnwood, Illinois USA

This edition first published in 1992 by Passport Books,
Trade Imprint of NTC Publishing Group, 4255 West Touhy Avenue,
Lincolnwood (Chicago), Illinois 60646-1975 U.S.A.

© Maps and text Duncan Petersen Publishing Ltd 1992

Conceived, edited and designed by
Duncan Petersen Publishing Ltd,
54, Milson Road,
London W14 OLB

Filmset by SX Composing, Rayleigh, Essex
Printed by Mateu Cromo, Madrid, Spain

Cover photo: French Government Tourist Office

Every reasonable care has been taken to ensure the information in this
guide is accurate, but the publishers and copyright holders can accept no
responsibility for the consequences of errors in the text or on the maps,
especially those arising from closures, or those topographical changes
occurring after completion of the aerial survey on which the maps are based.

ACKNOWLEDGEMENTS

The author found the following books and other publications particularly helpful in her research:

A Paris (Guides Hachette Visa); Geoffrey Brereton, *A Short History of French Literature* (Penguin); *Guide de Paris mystérieux* (Tchou); *Guide des Parcs et Jardins de Paris* (Horay); *Le Guide du Routard Paris* (Hachette); J. Hillairet, *Connaissance du Vieux-Paris*, 3 vols (Gonthier/Editions de Minuit); *Lever de Rideau* (catalogue of theatre exhibition at the Bibliothèque Fornay, Paris); Ian Littewood, *Paris: A Literary Companion* (John Murray); Vivienne Menkes-Ivry, *Paris* (Helm French Regional Guides); Ian Nairn, *Nairn's Paris* (Penguin); *Paris Guide Vert* (Michelin); Georges Poisson, *Guide des Statues de Paris* (Hazan); Ian Robertson, *Blue Guide*, Paris, and *Environs* (A & C Black/W.W. Norton).

Editorial

Editorial director	Andrew Duncan
Assistant editor	Kate Macdonald
Index	Rosemary Dawe

Design

Art director	Mel Petersen
Designers	Chris Foley and Beverley Stewart

Aerial survey by Institut Géographique National, Paris
Maps created by Richard David Creative, 77, Leonard Street, London EC2A 4QS

Contents

About this book

How the mapping was made

Isometric mapping is produced from aerial photographic surveys. For this book, aerial photography was provided from the archives of the Institut Géographique National.

Scores of enlargements were made from the negatives, which Richard David Creative, a group of technical illustrators in London (address on page 5), then used to create the maps. It took well over 1,000 hours to complete the task.

'Isometric' projection means that verticals are the same height, whether in the foreground or the background – at the 'front' (bottom) of the page or at the 'back' (top). Thus the diminishing effect of perspective is avoided and all the buildings, whether near or distant, are shown in similar detail and appear at an appropriate height.

The order of the maps

The map squares are arranged in sequence running from north to south and from west to east. For further details, see the master location maps on pages 10-11.

Numerals on maps

Each numeral on a map cross refers to the text printed down the right hand border of the map. The numbers generally read from the top left of each map to the bottom right, in a west-east direction. However, there are deviations from this pattern when several interesting features occur close together, or within one street.

Opening and closing times

If a museum, display or exhibition is open during regular working hours, opening and closing times are not mentioned in the text accompanying the maps. Brief details are however given when opening times are irregular. In the case of historic or otherwise interesting buildings, assume that you cannot gain access to the interior unless opening times are mentioned.

Prices

F   means one person can eat a three-course meal for less than 120 francs.

FF   means one person can eat a three-course meal for less than 250 francs.

FFF   means one person can eat for less than 350 francs.

FFFF   means one person generally pays more than 350 francs. Wine is not included.

Hotel Prices

F   means a double room without breakfast costs less than 175 francs a head.

FF   means the same type of room costs less than 300 francs a head.

FFF   means the same type of room costs less than 55 francs a head.

FFFF   means the same type of room costs more than 500 francs a head.

Coverage

No guide book can cover everything of interest in Paris. This one contains a particularly wide range of information, and the writers concentrated on aspects of the city brought out by the special nature of the mapping, with emphasis on historical or general information that helped explain the fabric, evolution and working of the city. They have also tended to draw attention to the outstanding, even the peculiar, sometimes at the expense of the obvious and well-established, in the belief that this best reveals the essential character of a city. There is, in addition, much about eating, drinking, shopping and other practical matters.

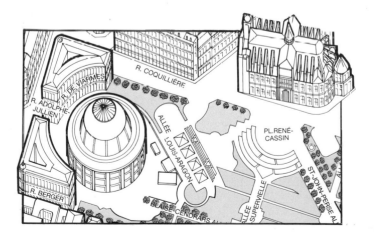

Master location map

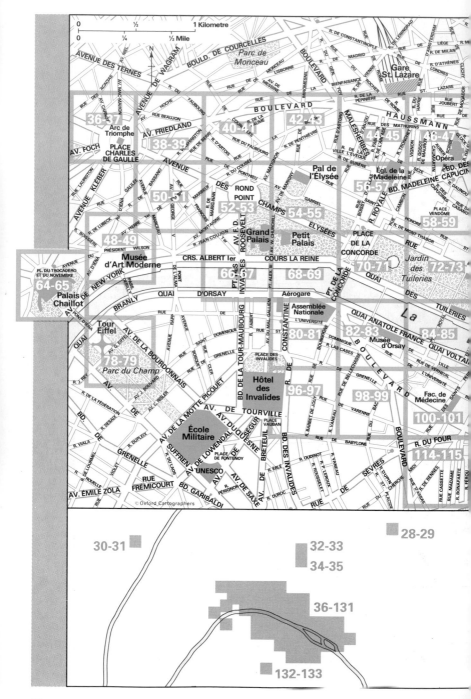

Gare du Nord

RUE LOUIS BLANC

Gare
de l'Est

Hôpital
St. Louis

BD. MONTMARTRE
D. DES ITALIENS

BOULD.
POISSONNIÈRE

BD. BONNE
NOUVELLE

PLACE
DE LA
RÉPUBLIQUE

. DU 4er SEPT

BD. DENIS

BD. ST. MARTIN

60-61

R. ST. AUGUSTIN

Bourse

62-63

RUE

RÉAUMUR

Bibliot.
Nation

Conserv.
Nat. Arts
et Metiers

R.   RÉAUMUR   TURBIGO

Jardin du
Palais Royal

74-75

76-77

Forum

Palais
Royal

Centre
National
d'Art

92-93

86-87

Palais
Louvre

RIVOLI

88-89

90-11

94-95

Archives
Nationales

QUAI DU LOUVRE

QUAI DE LA
MÉGISSERIE

RUE

RIVOLI

eine

École
eaux Arts

Q. DE CONTI

104-105

Palais de
Justice

Hôtel
de
Ville

Place
des
Vosges

102-103

Prefect.
de
Police

106-107

108-109

110-111

112-113

PLACE
DE LA
BASTILLE

SAINT

116-117

118-119

Notre
Dame

120-121

122-123

124-125

alais du
uxembourg
(Sénat)

Sorbonne

128-129

130-131

Université
Paris

126-127

Jardin du
uxembourg

Panthéon

Jardin
Plantes

28-29

30-31

La Défense

BOUL.CIRCULAIRE

132-133

Gare
Montparnasse

32-33

Sacre
Coeur

34-35

B.D.ROCHECHOUART

Transport

From airports to city

Passengers travelling into central Paris from Charles-de-Gaulle (CDG) airport (invariably referred to by Parisians as Roissy, the name of the nearest village) have a choice between Air France coach, shuttle bus plus express Métro (underground/subway) and ordinary bus.

Air France coaches operate between 5.45 am and 11 pm daily, with departures every 20 minutes from terminal CDG1 to avenue MacMahon (near the place Charles-de-Gaulle/Etoile) and the air terminal at the place de la Porte-Maillot; every 15 minutes from terminals CDG2A, 2B and 2D to the Porte Maillot and the avenue Carnot, again near the place Charles-de-Gaulle/Etoile. From these arrival points you can travel to your hotel by Métro (underground/subway), by RER (express Métro), by ordinary bus or by taxi. Journey time is at least 35 minutes and can be over an hour during the rush hours, especially on Friday evenings.

Free shuttle buses leave at frequent intervals from all four terminals for Roissy-Rail station, where you can take the RER to the Gare du Nord, Châtelet-Les Halles and any other station on the B line, which connects with the ordinary Métro; this method is not suitable if you have a lot of luggage. Ordinary bus No. 350 runs from the airport to the Gare de l'Est daily between 7 am and about 12.30 am; No. 351 to the place de la Nation daily between 7 am and about 8.30 pm. Taxis for the 25 km journey to central Paris cost about F200.

From Orly airport the choice is again between Air France coach, shuttle bus plus RER and ordinary bus.

Air France coaches depart from Orly-Ouest domestic terminal and Orly-Sud international terminal for the Gare Montparnasse and the Gare des Invalides every 12 minutes between 5.50 am and 11 pm; buses will stop at the

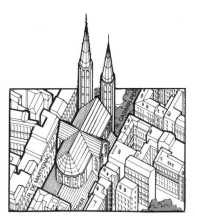

Porte d'Orléans and Duroc Métro station on request. Journey time Orly-Invalides is at least 30 minutes, more during rush hours. Shuttle buses marked Orly-Rail run from both terminals to Pont-de-Rungis/Aéroport d'Orly station on the C2 line of the RER; trains run at 15-minute intervals to the Gare d'Austerlitz, Pont-St-Michel, Musée d'Orsay and out to Versailles; again connections can be made to the ordinary Métro, but this method is best avoided if you have a lot of luggage. Ordinary buses, labelled Orlybus, run from about 7 am to 12.30 am at 15 minute intervals to place Denfert-Rochereau. Taxis for the 10 mile (16 km) journey into central Paris cost about F150.

Geography

Paris is divided into twenty districts, known as *arrondissements*. They are called *le premier* (written 1er), *le deuxième* (written 2e), *le troisième* (written 3e) and so on. If you write to one of the establishments mentioned in this guide, you must use the Paris code 75 plus one or two zeros and the district number. Thus 2e becomes 75002 Paris; 15e, 75015 Paris.

A street gazetteer with individual maps for each district makes a useful complement to this guide; ask for the *Plan de Paris par arrondissement* at bookshops, news-stands and some cafés.

Travelling in Paris

The RATP (Paris Transport Authority) operates an efficient and fully integrated network of underground/subway trains, buses and express trains running out into the suburbs. Look out for route-finder machines providing information on the quickest way to reach your destination by whatever combination of transport suits you. Punch in the relevant data and out will come full details of how to proceed.

The Métro

Paris's underground or subway system, officially the *Métropolitain* but universally referred to as the Métro, is rightly admired. Service is fast and frequent (trains run at 90 second intervals for much of the day); trains are generally clean and comfortable; and security, once a problem, is now much improved, with police patrols common at major interchanges. Smoking is banned throughout the network. The service starts at about 5.15 am (a little later on Sunday) and ends at about 1.15 am. Lines are officially numbered but are commonly known by the names of the station at either end of the route. These termini are also used on the orange signs indicating a connection to another line (*correspondance*). The system is easily mastered and clear maps in various formats are available at all Métro stations and at tourist offices. As stations are close together and few are far underground, you will find the Métro a convenient way of getting about even for short hops.

The express network

Paris also has a three-line express system, the Réseau Express Régional (RER). The three lines, called A, B and C, are fully integrated into the Métro network but stretch far out into the suburbs, where they run overground, and sometimes operate in parallel with SNCF (ordinary rail) suburban services. They provide a fast way of getting across Paris, of getting out to the airports and of reaching interesting towns close to Paris such as Versailles or St-Germain-en-Laye. Maps are again available from Métro stations and tourist offices.

Buses

The existence of bus lanes on many routes in central Paris means that buses move reasonably fast, except during the evening rush hour (about 6 to 8). They are a good way of seeing Paris, with some positively scenic routes, such as the 24, which takes in the Madeleine, the place de la Concorde, the Louvre, the Pont Neuf, Notre Dame and the Latin Quarter. Montmartre has its own service, the *Montmartrobus*.

All buses operate a daytime service from 7 am to about 8.30 pm Mon-Sat, but only about twenty lines run on Sundays. Some of these also operate an evening service through to about 12.30 am. And ten *Noctambus* lines, appropriately indicated by an owl sign, radiate out from the place du Châtelet between 1.30 and 5.30 am every night. Clear route plans are posted up at bus stops and full bus maps, with lists of evening and Sunday services, are available from Métro stations and tourist offices.

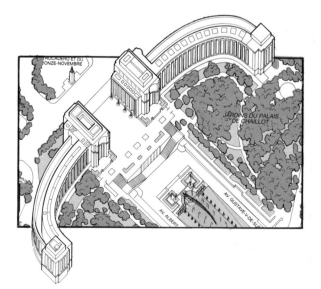

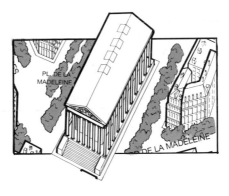

Tickets

The ticketing system for public transport is pleasantly straightforward and fares are generally good value. The same yellow tickets are used for both buses and the Métro. They are most economically bought in blocks of ten (ask for a *carnet*), but single tickets are also available. You can choose be tween first- and second-class tickets, but if you are planning to travel mostly by bus there is no point in paying first-class prices: buses have no first-class sections. Tickets are bought from the ticket window at Métro sta tions, from the cigarette counter in cafés sporting the RATP logo, or from slot machines at some stations and outside some major tourist sights.

One ticket allows you to travel anywhere on the ordinary Métro network, making as many changes as you like. Bus journeys require one, two or occasionally as many as four tickets (on the PC or *Petite Ceinture* that runs right round the city, and on some lines travelling into the suburbs). Check route maps at bus stops to see how many tickets you need for your journey. Short trips by RER within the city limits are paid for with the same tickets as for buses and the Métro. If you are travelling outside the city you must buy the appropriate ticket from a slot machine or a ticket window. All tickets must be slotted into machines on stations or at the entrance to buses: inspectors make frequent appearances and anyone without a valid punched ticket is liable to be fined.

Special tickets and passes

Tourist tickets (called *Formule 1* for a single day, or *Paris Sésame* for specific numbers of consecutive days) are good value. So is the *Carte Orange* season ticket, for which you buy weekly or monthly coupons covering the appropriate number of zones; passport-sized photographs are required.

Transport information

You can obtain information on all RATP services by dialling (1) 43 46 14 14 between 6 am and 9 pm.

Taxis

Paris taxis are ordinary saloon cars, whose drivers' knowledge of the city ranges from excellent to virtually non-existent. In theory they can be hailed in the street when their light is on. In practice few taxi drivers like plying for hire and you will save time by making for a taxi rank. Taxis waiting at ranks at rail stations make a special charge on top of the ordinary metred fare.

Metre rates are more expensive between 7.30 pm and 7 am and at all times on Sundays and public holidays, and when you travel outside the city limits. It is standard practice to add a tip of 10-15 per cent on top of the fare. Few drivers will take a passenger in the front seat, which limits you to three adults per cab; if a fourth person is allowed in, an extra charge will be made. Taxis can be ordered by telephone: ask your hotel to call one for you, or look in the telephone directory for the number of the nearest rank. Up-to-date numbers (they change frequently) of taxi companies and ranks are also listed most weeks in the 'What's on' weekly *Pariscope*.

Unlicensed taxis are often to be seen outside rail stations and major tourist sights. They are best avoided, as prices are steep and drivers may not be fully insured. If you are desperate and cannot afford to wait in the queue for licensed taxis, always agree the price before getting in to a private cab.

Private cars

Driving in Paris is not recommended for those unfamiliar with the city. The inhabitants are not known for their courtesy to other road users and become notoriously aggressive when hunting for a parking space. Parking close to museums and main sights is rarely feasible, the narrow streets in the city centre offer few parking opportunities and the 'Denver boot' (wheel clamp) is frequently used. If you must have a car in Paris, ask at a tourist information centre for a map showing paying car-parks (mostly underground), then use the excellent public transport for getting around within the city, and restrict your driving to Sundays and excursions outside Paris.

Speed limits in France: 60 kmph (or occasionally 50 – look for signs) in built-up areas, 90 kph on ordinary roads elsewhere, 130 kmph on motorways.

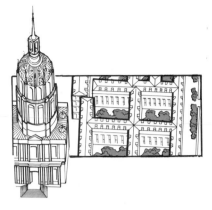

Useful data

Tourist information

The main Paris tourist office (*Office du Tourisme et des Congrès de Paris*) is at:

- 127 avenue des Champs-Elysées, 8e, tel: (1) 47 23 61 72; open daily 9 am to 8 pm

Additional information bureaux at:

- Gare du Nord, international arrivals concourse: open 1 May 31 Oct, Mon-Sat 8 am to 10 pm, Sun 1 pm to 8 pm; rest of year Mon-Sat only, 8 am to 8 pm.
- Gare de l'Est, arrivals concourse: open 1 May-31 Oct, Mon-Sat 8 am to 10 pm; rest of year Mon-Sat, 8 am to 8 pm.
- Gare d'Austerlitz, main line arrivals concourse: open 1 May-31 Oct, Mon-Sat 8 am to 10 pm; rest of year, Mon-Sat 8 am to 3 pm.
- Gare de Lyon, by exit from main line section: open 1 May-31 Oct, Mon-Sat 8 am to 10 pm; rest of year, Mon-Sat 8 am to 8 pm.
- Eiffel Tower: open May-Sept only, daily 11 am to 6 pm.

   The main office has a large number of leaflets on tourist sights and events and can make hotel bookings (for a small fee) for the next few days; at the other bureaux bookings can normally be made only for the same day. Be prepared for long queues at the main office at Easter and at the height of the summer season.

   Recorded information on entertainment and one-off sporting and leisure events can be obtained by dialling the *Sélection Loisirs* service: in French (1) 47 20 94 94; in English (1) 47 20 88 98; in German (1) 47 20 57 58.

   Annually updated booklets listing all hotels affiliated to the Paris tourist office can be obtained by writing to the main office, which also publishes a calendar showing when accommodation is likely to be hard to come by (because of trade fairs, conferences and the like).

Publications

Paris has two 'What's On' weeklies, *Pariscope* and *L'Officiel des Spectacles*, both published on Wednesday and available from news-stands. They are essential reading for checking current museum opening times, and also provide a wealth of information on entertainment and leisure and cultural or sporting events. The free monthly *Paris Sélection*, available from most hotels, lists events and facilities geared to tourists.

Sightseeing tours

Coach tours of Paris and the surrounding area are organized by:

■ Cityrama, 4 place des Pyramides, 1er, tel: (1) 42 60 30 14.

■ Paris Vision, 214 rue de Rivoli, 1er, tel: (1) 42 60 30 01 or (1) 42 60 31 25.

Bookings can be made directly with the companies or through your hotel.

The RATP also has an excursion service covering the Île-de-France region round Paris, using ordinary buses rather than luxury coaches. Bookings can be made at the two excursion offices:

■ place de la Madeleine, 8e (on the east side of the church, by the flower market).

■ 53 quai des Grands-Augustins, 6e.

Lecture tours of châteaux and other historic buildings near Paris are organized by the Caisse Nationale des Monuments Historiques (Hôtel de Sully, 62 rue St-Antoine, 4e), which publishes a *Bulletin des Musées & Monuments Historiques* every two months, and by a number of private companies. Details are given in the two 'What's On' weeklies, and in the newspapers *Le Monde* and *Le Figaro*. Commentary is only in French.

PL. VENDÔME

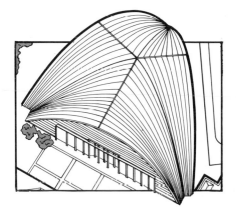

River trips Sightseeing cruises on the Seine are run by:
- Bateaux-Mouches (boats leave from Right Bank end of Pont de l'Alma); tel: (1) 42 25 96 10.
- Bateaux Parisiens – Tour Eiffel (boats leave from Left Bank end of Pont d'Iéna); tel: (1) 47 05 50 00.
- Bateaux Vedettes du Pont Neuf (boats leave from square du Vert-Galant, beside the Pont Neuf); tel: (1) 46 33 98 38.
- Vedettes de Paris (boats leave from Port de Suffren); tel: (1) 47 05 71 29 or (1) 45 50 23 79.

Most of these companies run special lunch and dinner cruises; advance booking and respectable dress essential. All cruises have a commentary in various languages, sometimes taped, sometimes by a live hostess.

You can also use the Seine as a means of transport by using the *Batobus* service: regular boats ply up and down the river at half-hourly intervals from 10 am to 7 pm daily during the tourist season, with five embarkation and disembarkation points (Eiffel Tower, the Musée d'Orsay, the Passerelle des Arts, Notre Dame and the Hôtel de Ville).

Canal cruises Trips along the Canal Saint-Martin to the Bassin de la Villette, sometimes combined with a brief cruise along the Seine, are run by:
- Canauxrama: tel: (1) 42 39 15 00.
- Paris Canal: tel: (1) 42 40 96 97.

Advance bookings essential, as the boats are quite small. Cruises last about 3 hours; evening cruises with a jazz band are also on offer.

Cruises on the Canal de l'Ourcq and to places like Monet's house at Giverny in Normandy are run by:
- Quiztour: tel: (1) 45 26 16 59.

Helicopter trips For a bird's eye view of Paris:
- Hélifrance: tel: (1) 45 54 95 11; (departures from the Paris Héliport, 4 avenue de la Porte-de-Sèvres, 15e).

Walking tours Lecture tours of specific districts on foot, or on specific themes, including visits to exhibitions, museums and other places of interest, are run year-round by the Caisse Nationales des Monuments Historiques (see above), by various private companies and by some individual guides. Look for the week's programme in the 'What's On' publications.

Museums and other places of interest

Virtually all museums and many other tourist sights charge an entrance fee, though this may be waived on Sundays. Reductions may be allowed to senior citizens, children, students, teachers, journalists and professional artists. Take along your passport to prove your age where relevant, and professional identification if you are in one of the favoured categories. Opening hours are a jungle. State-run museums (*musées nationaux*) shut on Tuesdays, City of Paris museums on Mondays, private museums often on Sundays. Lunchtime closures are common, even at the height of the tourist season, and opening times may vary when a temporary exhibition is being staged. Decisions on whether or not to close on a public holiday are often taken at the last minute. It is therefore essential to check current opening times in the list in one of the 'What's On' weeklies.

Evening opening, for instance at the Beaubourg/Pompidou Centre, the Louvre and the Grand Palais, is a help in avoiding the crowds. Wednesday afternoons (half-day holidays for schools) are best avoided in term-time.

Museum passes You can save money and avoid tedious queuing by buying a *Carte Musées*, valid for a single day, or for three or five consecutive days, in 60 major museums and places of interest in and around Paris, including Versailles. Available from Métro stations and in major museums.

Churches Churches are usually open early (from about 7 am) but close for several hours at lunchtime (from 12.30), then open again till about 7 pm. Visits are curtailed on Sunday mornings and when other masses are held.

Shopping, banking and business hours

Small food shops typically open at about 8 am (earlier for bakeries), close for lunch between about 1 and 3.30 or 4, then reopen till 7.30 or 8. Many are open on Sunday mornings but shut on Mondays. Open-air food markets, held all over Paris, are usually open mornings only, two or three days a week, often including Sundays. Supermarkets, department stores and other large shops open from about 9 am to 7 pm (Mon-Sat), with late-night opening at least one day a week in the case of department stores. Small fashion and gift boutiques, art galleries and antique shops may not open until as late as 11 or 12 and usually shut for at least an hour for lunch, possibly between 2 and 3 to catch the trade from office workers in their lunch hours.

Banking hours are roughly 9 to 4.30, but exchange counters (which are surprisingly few and far between in Paris) may well shut between 12 and 2. All banks close at lunchtime the day before a public holiday.

Exchange counters operate at Orly and Roissy/CDG airports daily from about 6 am to 11.30 pm and at the Gare de Lyon from about 6 am to 11 pm. Also open daily, but for shorter hours, bank branches at the Austerlitz, Est, Nord and St-Lazare rail stations. The UBP at 154 avenue des Champs-Elysées, 8e, is open at weekends from about 10.30 am to 6 pm, and the *Crédit Commercial de France* (CCF) at no. 117 is open Mon-Sat from 8 am to 8 pm. Cash dispensers (*billetteries*) enabling you to draw cash on a Visa card and some other international credit cards are found all over the city.

Private bureaux de change, usually offering less favourable rates, are particularly common in the St-Germain-des-Près district.

Office hours are 8.30 or 9 to 6 or 6.30, but many executives stay at work until at least 7. The evening rush hour therefore lasts from about 6 to 8. The morning rush hour, not usually quite as congested, is from about 7 to 9. As large numbers of Parisians have weekend homes outside Paris, roads out of the capital on Friday evenings are best avoided, and so are roads in on Sunday evenings.

Public holidays

Many museums and tourist sights and most shops are shut on: New Year's Day, Easter Monday, 1 May (Labour Day), 8 May (VE Day), Feast of the Ascension, Whit Monday, 14 July (national holiday to commemorate the storming of the Bastille), 15 August (Feast of the Assumption of the Virgin Mary), 1 November (All Saints), 11 November (Remembrance or Armistice Day), Christmas Day.

Annual holidays Most shops and restaurants close for several weeks for staff holidays, usually somewhere between 1 July and 15 September, though closure during the half-term holidays in February is also common. The theatre season is roughly October to the end of June, though a few, mainly small, theatres stay open during the summer.

Restaurants

It is possible to get a meal at most times of day in cafés and brasseries, but ordinary restaurants, whether small local places or grand gourmet high-spots, have fairly rigid mealtimes: lunch starts at about 12 and it is quite hard to find somewhere willing to take you after 1 or 1.15; dinner is served from 8 (earlier in places frequented by foreign tourists) and last orders may be as early as 9.30. Most restaurants are closed for at least one day a week, as well as observing a month-long summer closure.

Post

Post offices are open from 8 am to 7 pm Mon-Fri, 8-12 on Sat, and at least one post office in each *arrondissement* is open 8 am to midday on Sundays. The city's main post office, at 52 rue du Louvre, 1er, is open round-the-clock seven days a week. Stamps can be bought at post offices and from the cigarette counter in cafés marked with a red TABAC sign outside.

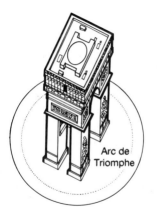

Arc de Triomphe

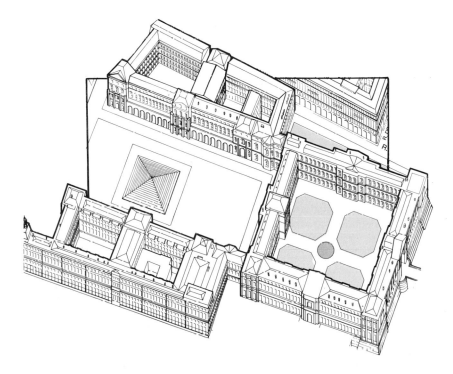

Telephoning

Telephone booths in the street, at stations and airports and in other public places take either coins or phonecards (*télécartes*), which can be bought from post offices and the cigarette counter in some cafés. International calls can be made from most public telephones; clear instructions in several languages are posted up in booths in major tourist areas.

All telephone numbers in France now consist of eight digits: there are no area codes except for Paris, whose numbers (all beginning with 4) must be preceded by 1 if you are telephoning from outside the capital. Calls from Paris to suburban numbers beginning with 3 or 6 require no prefix. To make a call from Paris to the provinces, dial 16, wait for a second tone, then dial the subscriber's eight-figure number. To make an international call, dial 19, wait for the second tone, then dial the country code, the area or city code and the number. The country code for France, which you must use if you are dialling one of the numbers given in this guide from abroad, is 33.

The Paris telephone directory is now published in three volumes. Yellow Pages volumes are also published. There is no operator service in France, but you can dial 12 for directory inquiries. For international directory inquiries dial 19, wait for the second tone, then dial 33 followed by the relevant country code.

Paris for children

The Jardin d'Acclimatation, on the Neuilly side of the Bois de Boulogne, Paris's main lung, is a lively mix of menagerie, miniature farm complete with goats and hens, funfair, miniature golf course and a children's museum (Musée en herbe) with regular painting workshops. You can even take children there on a little train from the Porte Maillot. And a short walk away, the Musée des Arts et Traditions Populaires (folk art and customs museum) is satisfyingly full of things to pull and push, as well as a collection of toys. Toys again feature in a new section in the Musée des Arts Décoratifs (applied arts museum, see page 73), and the Conservatoire des Arts et Métiers (craftsmanship and technology museum) has the tiny plane in which Blériot crossed the Atlantic, along with model trains, cars and aeroplane components.

Paris now has two science museums, the traditional Palais de la Découverte, with its popular planetarium, and, somewhat eclipsing it these days, the futuristic Cité des Sciences in the Parc de la Villette, a vast park offering many activities for children (see page 29).

On the eastern fringe of the city, the Bois de Vincennes has a full-scale zoo, and children also enjoy the little menagerie in the Jardin des Plantes on the edge of the Latin Quarter. Other parks where children can work off their surplus energy are the Parc Monceau, north of the Champs-Elysées, the romantically hilly Parc des Buttes-Chaumont in the north-east, and the Parc Montsouris and the newly laid out Parc Georges Brassens in the south, all of which offer various activities. Puppet and Punch & Judy shows are staged for most of the year in the Jardin du Luxembourg (see pages 126-27) and in the Champ de Mars (near the Eiffel Tower, see page 79), which also offers donkey rides, a popular treat also available in the Jardin des Tuileries (see page 72), with its famous ornamental pool for sailing boats.

Foreign embassies

Embassies and consulates are listed in the telephone directory under *Ambassade* and *consulat*. Here is a selection:

- **Australia** 4 rue Jean-Rey, 15e; tel: (1) 40 59 33 00.
- **Canada** 35 avenue Montaigne, 8e; tel: (1) 47 23 01 01.
- **Germany** 13 avenue Franklin-D.-Roosevelt, 8e; tel: (1) 42 99 78 00.
- **Great Britain** 35 rue de Faubourg-St-Honoré, 8e; tel: (1) 42 66 91 42.
- **Ireland** 4 rue Rude, 16e; tel: (1) 45 00 20 87.
- **Italy** 47 rue de Varenne, 7e; tel: (1) 45 44 38 90.
- **Japan** 7 avenue Hoche, 8e; tel: (1) 47 66 02 22.
- **Netherlands** 7 rue Eblé, 7e; tel: (1) 43 06 61 88.
- **New Zealand** 7ter rue Léonard-de-Vinci, 16e; tel: (1) 45 00 24 11.
- **Spain** 13 avenue George-V, 8e; tel: (1) 47 23 61 83.
- **USA** 2 avenue Gabriel, 8e; tel: (1) 42 96 12 02 or (1) 42 61 80 75.

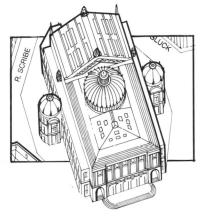

Emergencies

Police Secours (accidents): dial 17.
Fire brigade: dial 18.

Medical emergencies:

- SAMU (first aid in accidents): tel: dial 15 or (1) 45 67 50 50.
- SOS Médecins: tel: (1) 47 07 77 77.
- SOS Dentistes (dental emergencies): tel: (1) 43 37 51 00.
- Poisoning emergencies: tel: (1) 40 37 04 04 0.
- Blood transfusions: tel: (1) 43 07 47 28.
- A.P. Ambulances: tel: (1) 43 78 26 26.
- Serious burns (adults): Hôpital Cochin, rue du Faubourg- St-Jacques, 14e, tel. (1) 42 34 17 58; Hôpital St-Antoine, rue du Faubourg-St-Antoine, 12e, tel. (1) 49 28 20 00; (children); Hôpital Trousseau, avenue du Docteur-Arnold-Netter, 12e, tel. (1) 43 46 13 90.

Late-night chemists

Paris has one 24-hour chemist, the Pharmacie Dhéry, 84 avenue des Champs-Elysées, 8e. The following are open until 1 am:

- Chemist's counter in Drugstore Publicis St-Germain, 149 boulevard St-Germain, 6e.
- Pharmacie Machelon, 5 place Pigalle, 9e.
- Pharmacie Opéra, 6 boulevard des Capucines, 2e.

Main police station

9 boulevard du Palais, 4e.

Lost property

Central office is at 36 rue des Morillons, 15e (open Mon, Tues, Wed and Fri, 8.30 am to 5 pm; Thurs, 8.30 am to 8 pm).

Paris Metro map

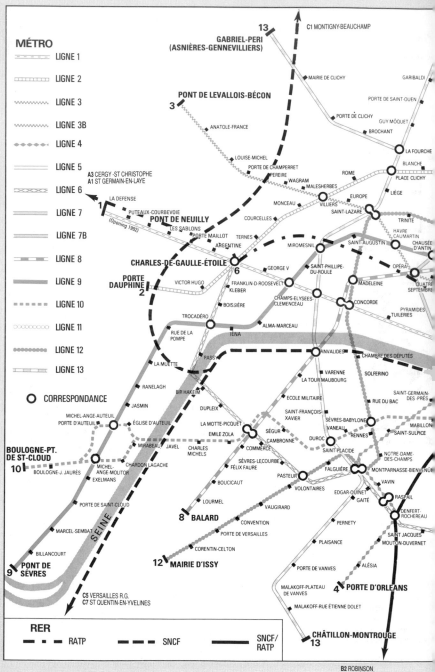

SAINT-DENIS BASILIQUE
(HÔTEL DE VILLE) 13

B3 ROISSY-AÉROPORT
CHARLES DE GAULLE
B5 MITRY-CLAYE

CARREFOUR PLEYEL   SAINT-DENIS
PORTE DE PARIS

MAIRIE DE SAINT-OUEN

LA COURNEUVE-8 MAI 1945 7

FORT-D'AUBERVILLIERS

AUBERVILLIERS-PANTIN 4 CHEMINS

PORTE DE CLIGNANCOURT 4

PORT DE LA CHAPELLE 12

PORTE DE LA VILLETTE

BOBIGNY-
PABLO PICASSO
(PRÉFECTURE-HÔTEL
DU DÉPARTEMENT)

SIMPLON

MARX-DORMOY

CORENTIN-CARIOU

JULES JOFFRIN
LAMARCK-
CAULAINCOURT   CHATEAU-ROUGE

MARCADET-POISSONNIERS

CRIMÉE

BOBIGNY-PANTIN
RAYMOND QUENEAU
ÉGLISE DE PANTIN 5

ABBESSES

ANVERS

LA CHAPELLE

RIQUET

PIGALLE

BARBÈS-
ROCHECHOUART

STALINGRAD

HOCHE

PORT DE PANTIN

SAINT-GEORGES

GARE DU NORD

LOUIS
BLANC
7B

JAURÈS

DURCQ

LAUMIÈRE

BUTTES-CHAUMONT

DANUBE

NOTRE-DAME-
DE-LORETTE

CHÂTEAU LANDON

BOLIVAR

BOTZARIS

PRÉ-ST-GERVAIS
7B

MAIRIE
DES LILAS
11

COLONEL FABIEN

PLACE DES FÊTES

LE PELETIER
RICHELIEU-DROUOT

CADET

POISSONNIÈRE

GARE DE L'EST

BELLEVILLE

PYRÉNÉES JOURDAIN

TÉLÉGRAPHE

PORTE
3B DES LILAS

CHATEAU D'EAU

JACQUES BONSERGENT

COURONNES

SAINT-FARGEAU

BONNE NOUVELLE

STRASBOURG-SAINT-
DENIS

GONCOURT

PELLEPORT

RUE
BOURSE   MONTMARTRE

SENTIER

RÉPUBLIQUE

PARMENTIER

MÉNILMONTANT

PORTE DE BAGNOLET

RÉAUMUR-SÉBASTOPOL

TEMPLE

SAINT MAUR

3B

GALLIENI 3

ÉTIENNE MARCEL

ARTS ET MÉTIERS

FILLES DU
CALVAIRE

OBERKAMPF

GAMBETTA

PALAIS-ROYAL

LOUVRE

LES HALLES

RAMBUTEAU

SAINT-SÉBASTIEN
FROISSART

SAINT-AMBROISE

PÈRE-LACHAISE

PONT NEUF

PHILIPPE AUGUSTE

VOLTAIRE

CHÂTELET 11

HÔTEL DE VILLE

CHEMIN-
VERT

RICHARD-
LENOIR

CHARONNE

ALEXANDRE-DUMAS

CROIX-DE-CHAVAUX
ROBESPIERRE 9

MAIRIE DE
MONTREUIL

SAINT PAUL

BRÉGUET-SABIN

PONT MARIE

CITÉ

PONT MARIE

BASTILLE

BOULETS
MONTREUIL

AVRON

PORTE DE MONTREUIL

A4 TORCY
MARNE-LA-VALLÉE
A2 BOISSY-ST-LÉGER

SULLY-MORLAND

LEDRU-ROLLIN

2

MARAÎCHERS

ODÉON

SAINT-MICHEL

FAIDHERBE-
CHALIGNY

NATION

BUZENVAL

PORTE DE VINCENNES

SAINT-MANDÉ-TOURELLE

CLUNY LA SORBONNE

6

BÉRAULT

MAUBERT-MUTUALITÉ

REUILLY-DIDEROT

PICPUS

CARDINAL LEMOINE

GARE DE LYON

CHÂTEAU DE VINCENNES 1

JUSSIEU

QUAI DE LA RÂPÉE

MONTGALLET

BEL-AIR

MONGE

DAUMESNIL

CENSIER-DAUBENTON

GARE D'AUSTERLITZ 10

DUGOMMIER

MICHEL BIZOT

SAINT MARCEL

BERCY

LES GOBELINS

QUAI DE LA GARE

CAMPO FORMIO

CHEVALERET

PORTE DORÉE

GLACIÈRE

CORVISART

5

NATIONALE

PLACE D'ITALIE

PORTE DE CHARENTON

LIBERTÉ

TOLBIAC

CHARENTON-ÉCOLES

ALFORT-ÉCOLE VÉTÉRINAIRE

MAISON BLANCHE

PORTE D'IVRY

SEINE

MAISONS-ALFORT-STADE

KREMLIN-BICÊTRE

PORTE DE CHOISY

PORTE D'ITALIE

PIERRE-CURIE

MAISONS-ALFORT-LES JUILLIOTTES

CRÉTEIL-L'ÉCHAT
(HOP. HENRI MONDOR)
CRÉTEIL-UNIVERSITÉ

VILLEJUIF-LÉO LAGRANGE

VILLEJUIF-PAUL VAILLANT COUTURIER

VILLEJUIF (LOUIS ARAGON) 7

MAIRIE D'IVRY 7

CRÉTEIL-PRÉFECTURE 8
(HÔTEL-DE-VILLE)

©Oxford Cartographers

C2 MASSY-PALAISEAU
C4 DOURDAN
C8 ST MARTIN D'ÉTAMPES

28

The Parc de la Villette

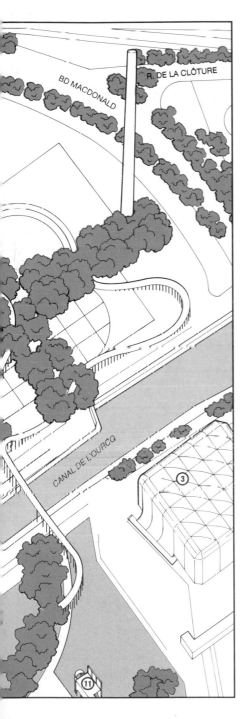

① Paris's exciting new 'Science City' (**Cité des Sciences et de l'Industrie**, closed Mon), a steel and glass structure completed in 1986 to prize-winning futuristic designs by French architect Adrien Fainsilber, is a far cry from the traditional science museum. Dubbed an 'interactive experience' – children are positively encouraged to touch (and to pull, push and otherwise manhandle) many of the exhibits – it includes a Planetarium, an 'Inventorium' (for children aged 3 to 12), a multimedia centre and a model of the Ariane space rocket. It was built on the foundations of the huge cattle auction building, a white elephant that was already obsolete when it was built at the end of the Sixties to replace part of the city's 19thC slaughter-houses and meat-market complex. ② Outside the main entrance is **La Géode**, a shiny steel sphere, also designed by Fainsilber, housing a popular cinema with a 1000 sq m (11,000 sq ft) hemispherical screen and an Omnimax 180-degree projection system. ③ **Le Zénith** stages pop and rock concerts. ④ The *Halle aux Boeufs* (cattle market), built in 1867 and the only survivor of the original three glass and cast-iron market buildings, has been splendidly refurbished and re-christened **La Grande Halle**. It is now used for large-scale entertainment (it can seat up to 16,000), exhibitions and trade fairs. ⑤ The **Théâtre Paris-Villette** stages mostly contemporary plays. On either side of ⑥ the **Fontaine aux Lions** (Lion Fountain), dating from the early 19thC and moved here in 1867 from what was to become the place de la République in eastern Paris, are the twin buildings forming ⑦ and ⑧, the **Cité de la Musique** (music academy plus concert hall and musical instrument museum, due to open in 1993. The park, Paris's largest, is dotted with ⑨–⑪ bright red **Folies** (follies), all variants on the theme of the cube, used to house an information centre, children's workshops and studios and a video gallery. ⑫ Children are also catered for by the brightly coloured **Dragon**, a giant slide made from scrap metal. ⑬ **Croixement (F)**, overlooking the Canal de l'Ourcq, is handy for drinks and light meals. ⑭ Close by is the **landing stage** for the boats that ply between the Parc de la Villette and the Bassin de la Villette marina, from where you can enjoy a 3-hour cruise in a canal boat back to central Paris (*see page 19*).

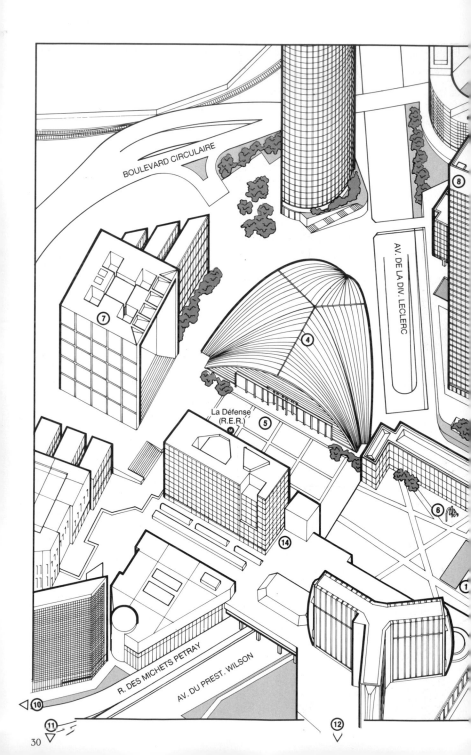

BOULEVARD CIRCULAIRE

AV. DE LA DIV. LECLERC

⑧

⑦

④

La Défense
(R.E.R.)
Ⓜ ⑤

⑥

⑭

①

R. DES MICHETS PETRAY

AV. DU PREST. WILSON

◁⑩

⑪

⑫

30

La Défense

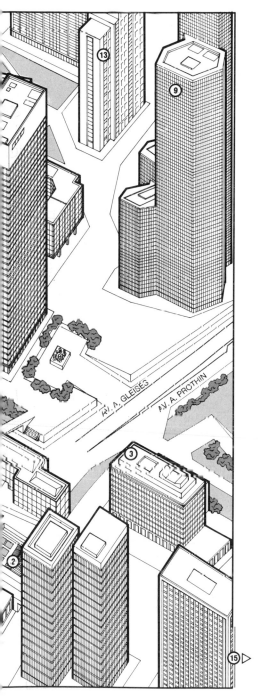

The high-rise business and residential district beyond Neuilly on Paris's western outskirts takes its name from ① a bronze **memorial to those who defended Paris during the Franco-Prussian War**. Unlike most of the work of its prolific 19thC sculptor Barrias, including a much-reviled statue of Victor Hugo in his eponymous square, it survived the Nazi occupation and is now back on its original site, though in a totally different setting. Close to it is ② the **Bassin Agam**, adorned with a fountain that erupts into life at intervals, to the accompaniment of *son-et-lumière* style lighting and music. And all round it tower the huge blocks that today form the western limit of the 'Triumphal Way' planned by Louis XIV and his master gardener André le Nôtre (*see page 73*). ③ The earliest of the 'Tours' (*tower blocks*) is the **Tour Esso**, dating from 1964. ④ The **CNIT**, the popular abbreviation of the Palais du Centre national des Industries et des Techniques, was opened the same year. An exhibition centre gradually being converted into an office complex and conference centre, it has a triangular roof, swooping down, like some vast concrete tent, to its three corners. In front of it, ⑤ a **sculpture by Joan Miró**, and nearby, ⑥ a bright-red **Stabile by Alexander Calder**. ⑦ The gigantic **Grande Arche**, a shiny concrete cube faced with glass and white marble and famously big enough for Notre Dame cathedral to fit inside it, was opened in 1909 to celebrate the bicentenary of the French Revolution, and houses among other things the International Foundation for Human Rights. ⑧ The **Tour Fiat**, one of Europe's tallest buildings, 770 feet/235 metres high, is the daytime home of some 4500 office workers, slightly more than ⑨ the **Tour Elf**, a complex of five separate tower blocks designed on the 'organ pipe' principle (i.e. in descending order of height). ⑩ The **Tour Pascal**, dating from 1983, is the headquarters of IBM Europe, one of many multinationals with offices at La Défense, while ⑪ **Défense 2000**, ⑫ **Eve** and ⑬ **Gambetta** are the three exceptions to the general rule that office blocks are higher-rise than residential complexes. ⑭ **Les Quatre Temps** is Europe's largest shopping centre. ⑮ La Défense is reached from Paris via the **Pont de Neuilly**, the second descendant of the bridge where in 1654 Blaise Pascal was involved in a carriage accident that, according to Voltaire, meant that the author of *Les Pensées* was no longer in his right mind.

Lamarck Caulaincourt

R. CAULAINCOURT

◁ (13)

PL. CONSTANTIN-
PECQUEUR

R. GIRARDON

R. LUCIEN-
GAULARD

R. GASTON-COUTÉ

R. PAUL-FEVAL

ALLÉE DES
BROUILLARD

R. ST-VINCENT

(10)

(12)

R. DES SAULES

R. GIRARDON

R. DE L'ABREUVOIR

(11)

(9)

(8)

R. CORTOT

(14)

R. NORVINS

(7)

R. ST-RUSTIQUE

R. LEPIC

R. NORVINS

R. D'ORCHAMPT

PL. JEAN-
BAPTISTE-
CLÉMENT

R. POULBOT

(3)

(4) (5)

(6)

R. RA[...]IGNAN

(16)

PL. EMILE-
GOUDEAU

R. GABRIELLE

R. DES TROIS-FRÈRES

(15)

R. ANDROUET

R. DU CALVAIRE

R. DURANTIN

R. BERTHE

R. DREVET

Montmartre

① The wedding cake silhouette of the **Sacré Coeur** basilica is visible from all over Paris. One of the city's best-known buildings, though certainly not the most aesthetically pleasing, it was built by public subscription as a symbol of expiation and renewed faith in the future after the traumatic defeat in the Franco-Prussian War. The interior, vast, impressive and always crowded, is dominated by a huge Byzantine-style mosaic of Christ. ② Incorporated in the walls of **St-Pierre-de-Montmartre**, once part of a huge abbey, and one of the few surviving Romanesque churches in Paris, are four marble columns, probably from one of the Roman temples built on this long-holy hill. ③ The **place du Tertre** is Tourist Montmartre with a vengeance: a picturesque village square now overrun with distinctly undistinguished artists busy at their easels. ④ **La Crémaillère 1900** (**FF**) at No. 15, with art nouveau-ish décor, is better than most of the mediocre but often entertaining restaurants in and around the square. ⑤ No. 6, a restaurant since 1793, is still called **Chez la Mére Catherine (FF)** in memory of its first *patronne*. ⑥ Next door at No. 4, **Au Cadet de Gascogne**, one of many atmospheric '*cabarets artistiques*' boasting live accordion music. ⑦ **A la Bonne Franquette**, on the corner of the villagey rue St-Rustique, is another – but with the distinction of featuring in a Van Gogh painting. ⑧ '**The Pink House**' has also been immortalized on canvas, this time by Utrillo, who lived briefly in what is now ⑨ the **Musée de Montmartre** (12 rue Cortot, closed Mon), set in a delightful little garden and full of exhibits redolent of the spirit of '*le Vieux Montmartre*'. ⑩ Utrillo is buried in the **Cimetière St-Vincent**. ⑪ The Butte Montmartre (Montmartre Hillock) was once covered with vines. In memory of this small **vineyard**, grandly called 'le Clos Montmartre', was planted in the thirties. ⑫ **Le Lapin Agile**, a pinky-red cottage with green shutters, was one of the high-spots of bohemian night life in the early years of this century and is still a good place to enjoy an evening of French songs and nostalgia (closed Mon). ⑬ **Clodenis** (**FF**, closed Sun and Mon), at 57 rue Caulaincourt, reliable cuisine away from the tourist hordes. ⑭ The **Moulin de la Galette**, famous from Renoir's painting, one of only two surviving windmills of the dozens whose sails used to whirl away on top of the hill. ⑮ See ①, ② and ③, page 34. ⑯ See ④, page 34.

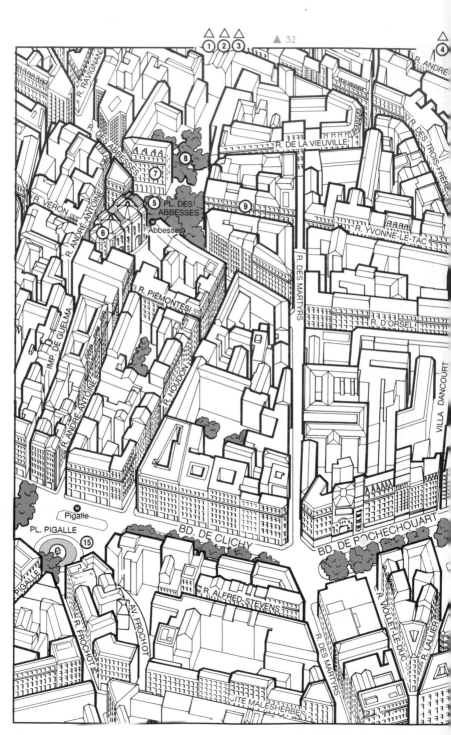

▲ 32

Montmartre

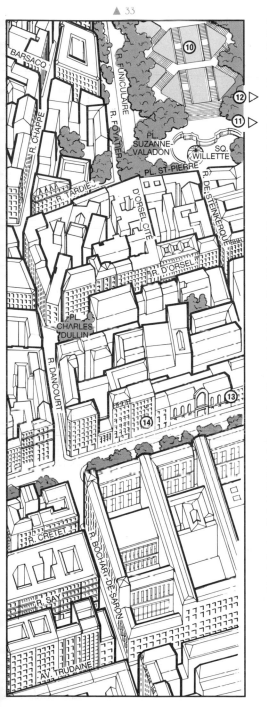

① The charming little **place Emile-Goudeau** (*see page 32*), adorned with one of the graceful green drinking fountains bequeathed to Paris by Sir Richard Wallace (off map), whose famous art collection formed the basis of London's Wallace Collection. ② At No. 13 the wooden **Bateau-Lavoir** (off map), home and studio of Picasso and Modigliani among many other artists (*Les Demoiselles d'Avignon* was painted there), has been rebuilt after being ravaged by a fire in 1970. ③ **Le Relais de la Butte** (**F**, closed Mon, and Tues for lunch in winter, off map), a cosy inn that dates back to the 17thC. ④ The tiny **place du Calvaire** (stunning views over Paris). ⑤ The **place des Abbesses** is a remainder of the abbey that once spread over the hill. ⑥ 'St-Jean-des-Briques' is the locals' irreverent nickname for the early 20thC church of **St-Jean-l'Evangéliste**, an early example of reinforced concrete construction, faced with brick. ⑦ Some of the rooms in the pleasant **Hôtel Régyn's Montmartre** (**FF**) at No. 18 overlook ⑧ the **square Jehan-Rictus**, previously the square Louis-XVI, where the bodies of Marie Antoinette and Louis XVI were originally taken from the guillotine for burial. ⑨ **St Denis** (whose martyrdom, along with two companions, may have given Montmartre its name as '*Mont des Martyrs*' or 'Martyrs' Mount') was allegedly beheaded in the rue **Yvonne-Le-Tac**, which also saw the founding, in 1534, of the Society of Jesus, by Ignatius Loyola. ⑩ The steep, zigzagging steps in the **square Willette** lead down from the Sacré-Coeur (*see page 33*) to ⑪ the 19thC **Halle-St-Pierre**, a market building converted into two museums, one devoted to naïve art, the other a children's museum, the Musée en Herbe, which also organizes workshops ⑫ The **Marché St Pierre**, a famous fabric market. ⑬ The **Théâtre Elyse-Montmartre** (72 boulevard de Rochechouart), originally a very popular dance hall, with a superb art nouveau façade. ⑭ **Le Chat Noir** (No. 84) became Paris's best-known cabaret thanks to the larger-than-life *chansonnier* Aristide Bruant, whose 'uniform' of black hat and red scarf is so familiar from Lautrec's poster. ⑮ **Place Pigalle**, the heart of a sleazy entertainment district.

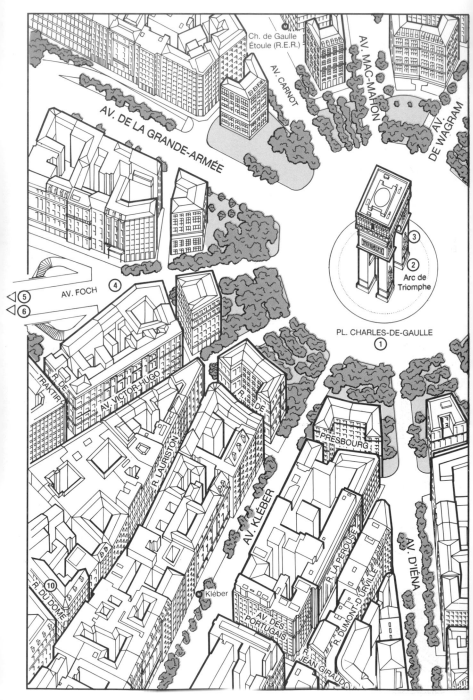

Ch. de Gaulle Étoule (R.E.R.)

AV. CARNOT

AV. MAC-MAHON

AV. DE WAGRAM

AV. DE LA GRANDE-ARMÉE

AV. FOCH

◁ 5
◁ 6
4

3
2
Arc de Triomphe

PL. CHARLES-DE-GAULLE
1

R. DE TRAKTIR

R. DE

AV. VICTOR-HUGO

R. LAURISTON

R. DE

PRESBOURG

AV. KLÉBER

R. LA PÉROUSE

AV. D'IÉNA

R. DU DOME
10

Kléber

AV. DES PORTUGAIS

R. DUMONT-D'URVILLE

R. JEAN GIRAUDOUX

The Etoile

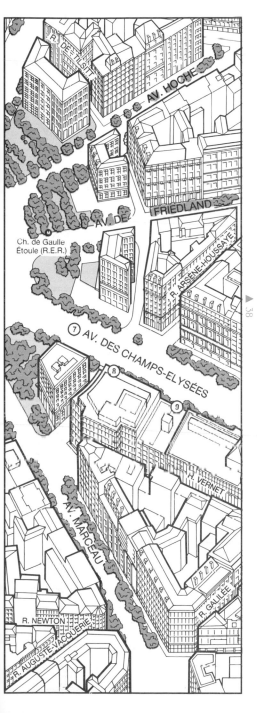

① The vast **place Charles-de-Gaulle**, with its twelve radiating avenues, has been officially so called since the General died in 1970. But it is still known to Parisians as '*L'Etoile*', The Star, an abbreviation of place de l'Etoile, the name used for it even before it was redesigned by Baron Haussmann, Prefect of the Seine in the 1850s and 1860s, whose grandiose town planning schemes had such a dramatic effect on the city. ② Dominating the square is the imposing bulk of Jean Chalgrin's **Arc de Triomphe**, planned by Napoleon Bonaparte as a monument to France's armed forces, but not completed until 1836, long after his death. When Napoleon married Marie Louise of Austria in 1810, the enterprising Chalgrin arranged for a canvas model, fastened to a wooden frame, to stand in for the future arch as a fitting backdrop to the celebrations. The arch has a little museum (closed public hols) and a platform offering splendid views. ③ The emotive *Departure of the Volunteers in 1792*, a superb set piece by the Romantic sculptor François Rude, is always known, for obvious reasons, as '*La Marseillaise*'. ④ The chic **avenue Foch**, lined with strips of lawn and elegant town houses, and leading straight to the Bois de Boulogne, is the widest of the Etoile's avenues. ⑤ The **Musée d'Ennery** (No. 59, open Sun and Thurs afternoons, off map), based on a collection of oriental art built up by Adolphe d'Ennery, a popular playwright specializing in melodramas. ⑥ Paris's large Armenian community likes visiting the **Musée Arménien** on the ground floor of Ennery's mansion (same opening days, off map). ⑦ Much the best known of the avenues, the **Champs-Elysées**, now flanked by sadly nondescript modern buildings, is still a byword abroad for Parisian glamour. In 1990 Mayor Jacques Chirac decreed a plan to beautify it with plants and specially designed street furniture. ⑧ **The Drugstore** (No. 133), a glossy French creation that bears little resemblance to its transatlantic model, is a popular place for golden youth to meet for a drink or a late-night meal, or to buy foreign papers and gimmicky gifts. ⑨ Paris's main **tourist office** (No. 127). ⑩ Baudelaire died in Dr Duval's hydro-therapy clinic in the **rue du Dôme**, paralysed and virtually speechless, on 31 August 1867. He was only forty-six.

R. BEAUJON

AV. BERTHIE ALBRECHT

PL. GEORGES-GUILLAUMIN

R. ARSÈNE-HOUSSAYE

R. BALZAC

R. LORD-BYRON

R. BALZAC

R. CHATEAUBRIAND

8

7

3

R. GALILÉE

George V

M

① AV. DES CHAMPS-ELYSÉES

R. VERNET

②

AV. GEORGE-V

R. DE BASSANO

R. EULER

R. QUENTIN BAUCHART

◀ 37

The Champs-Elysées

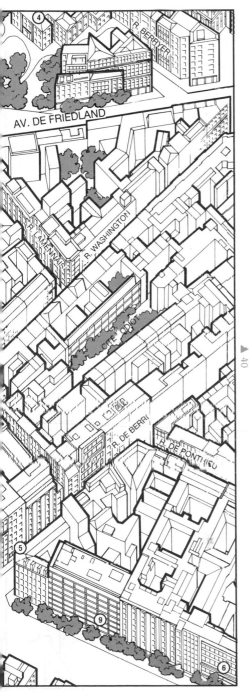

① The **avenue des Champs-Elysées** was designed by Louis XIV's master landscape gardener André Le Nôtre as the first section of a 'triumphal way' leading from the Tuileries Gardens (*see pages 72-3*) westwards to Versailles. Its sweeping uphill movement has long made it an ideal setting for processions, starting with the solemn return of Napoleon's remains from St Helena, on a bitterly cold day in December 1840, when a crowd of at least a hundred thousand braved ice and snow to catch a glimpse of the little coffin, draped in a long purple pall embroidered with gold bees. ② **Fouquet's** (**FF-FFF**, No. 99) has the most fashionable terrace on '*Les Champs*' and ③ **The Lido** (No. 116bis) its most lavish revues, famous for their fondness for feathers (and for acrobats, skaters, even live animals sometimes): very touristy, very expensive. ④ The **Hôtel Salomon de Rothschild** (11 rue Berryer) was the scene of the assassination of French president Paul Doumer on 6 May 1932, by a Russian *émigré* called Gorguloff. The superstitious like to point out that he was the country's thirteenth president, had been elected on 13 May and was struck down in his thirteenth month in office. ⑤ An inscription on **2 rue de Berri** tells you that another president, American this time, lived there when he was ambassador to Paris: Thomas Jefferson's residence from 1785 to 1789 was the Hôtel de Langeac, built by Chalgrin (architect of the Arc de Triomphe, *see page 37*), and one of dozens of opulent mansions then lining the Champs-Elysées and the surrounding streets. ⑥ **52-60 Champs-Elysées** is the site of another splendid mansion, the Hôtel de Massa, the first to be built on the avenue (as early as 1778); in 1928 it was dismantled and rebuilt near the Observatoire at 38 rue du Faubourg St-Jacques as a magnificent home for the Société des Gens de Lettres, France's authors' association. ⑦ The **Hôtel Balzac** (6 rue Balzac, **FFF**), one of the most charming of Paris's luxury hotels, has a conservatory-style restaurant, *Le Sallambier* (**FF**), with a good-value lunch menu. ⑧ Balzac died in a house on the site of **12 rue Balzac**. ⑨ The **Galerie des Champs**, the first of several deluxe shopping arcades off the north side of the Champs-Elyses.

▶ 40

▼ 51

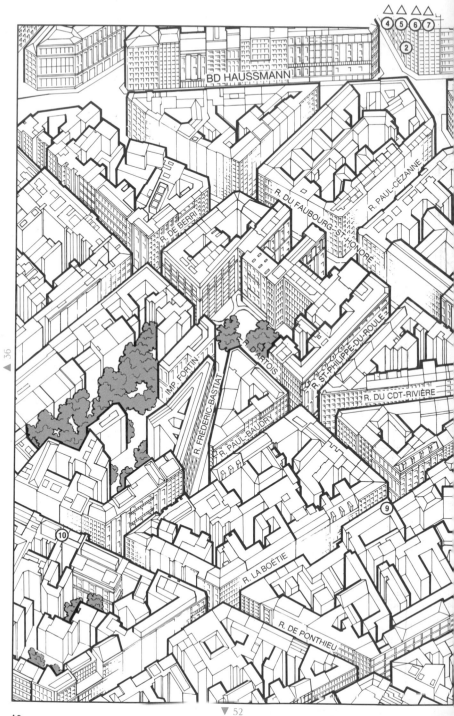

BD HAUSSMANN

R. DU FAUBOURG-ST-HONORÉ

R. PAUL-CÉZANNE

R. DE BERRI

R. ST-PHILIPPE-DU-ROULE

R. DU CDT-RIVIÈRE

IMP. FORTIN

R. D'ARTOIS

R. FRÉDÉRIC-BASTIAT

R. PAUL-BAUDRY

R. LA BOÉTIE

R. DE PONTHIEU

St-Philippe-du-Roule

① The **church of St-Philippe-du-Roule**, built to designs by Jean Chalgrin (who also designed the Arc de Triomphe, *see page 37*) between 1769 and 1784; with its portico of four Doric columns supporting a pediment, it was described in a book of drawings of Paris buildings by the architect Augustus Pugin as 'one of the best modern transcripts of the ancient Christian basilica'. ② Charles Dickens wrote of the death of little Paul Dombey when he was living with his family at **38 rue de Courcelles** in 1846; after starting *Dombey and Son* in Lausanne, he moved to Paris in November that year and was introduced to France's literary lions – Chateaubriand, Dumas, Lamartine and Hugo. ③ A grand 19thC mansion houses the rich collections of the **Musée Jacquemart-André**: 18thC paintings and furniture, and Quattrocento and Renaissance paintings from Italy, including important works by Uccello and Botticelli. ④ North of the museum, the **Parc Monceau** (off map), originally laid out a decade before the French Revolution for 'Philippe-Egalité', the father of King Louis Philippe, then replanned by Baron Haussmann in 1862, is a delightful park at the heart of a prosperous residential district: it boasts miniature lakes, artfully arranged ruins, a waterfall, a monument to Alfred de Musset by Antonin Mercié, originally in front of the Comédie française, and another by the same sculptor to the composer Charles Gounod, and ⑤ the circular **Pavillon de Chartres** (off map), one of the toll gates designed by Nicolas Ledoux in the 18thC for what became known as the 'Tax-collectors' Wall' (Mur des Fermiers-Généraux). On the edge of the park, two spacious mansions have been converted into museums: ⑥ the **Musée Cernuschi** (7 avenue Velasquez, off map) specializes in art from the Far East, especially China; ⑦ the **Musée Nissim-de-Camondo** (63 rue de Monceau, off map), full of elegant 18thC furniture and *objets d'art*. ⑧ The **rue du Colisée** takes its name from a vast entertainment centre on the site of No. 44, built in 1769 and consisting of shops, cafés and restaurants, public gardens, a lake, an orchestra – it was allegedly large enough to take up to forty thousand people. This and the surrounding streets are still a mecca for chic (and monied) nightlifers, who head in the early hours for ⑨ **Keur Samba** (79 rue La Botie) or ⑩ **Régine's** (49 rue de Ponthieu) or ⑪ **Olivia Valère** (40 rue du Colisée).

BD HAUSSMANN ⑨

⑪

R. DE LA BAUME

AV. PERCIER

Miromesnil Ⓜ

Mironesnil Ⓜ

R. LA BOÉTIE

①

AV. DELCASSÉ

R. DE MIROMESNIL

⑧

⑩

⑫

R. DE PENTHIÈVRE

⑦

③

②

R. DU FAUBOURG-ST-HONORÉ

AV. MATIGNON

R. DU CIRQUE

PL. BEAUVAU

④

▲ 41

La Boëtie

① The **Salle Gaveau** (45 rue La Boëtie) is one of Paris's major concert halls. ② The **Bristol** (**FFF**, 112 rue du Faubourg-St-Honoré), perhaps the most luxurious hotel in Paris, famous for its rooftop teak swimming-pool, its glamorous marble bathrooms, its magnificent panelled dining-room and huge formal garden (terrace for summer meals). ③ Books on fashion and costume, in several languages, are the speciality of **Jullien-Cornic** (29 avenue Matignon). ④ The circular **place Beauvau** takes its name from the Marquis de Beauvau, a Marshal of France, who commissioned ⑤ the **Hôtel Beauvau**, a grand 18thC mansion now housing the **Ministère de l'Intrieur** (Home Office/Interior Ministry), reached via elegant wrought-iron gates. ⑥ The **rue des Saussaies**, strange as it may seem in this traffic-ridden urban setting, led in the 18thC to a grove of weeping willows (*saussaie* in French); a far cry from this rural reminder, no. 11 was the headquarters of the Gestapo during the Second World War. ⑦ **Au Jardin du Printemps** (**FFF**, 32 rue de Penthièvre), undoubtedly the chic-est of Paris's Chinese restaurants. ⑧ The **rue de Laborde** commemorates Count Alexandre de Laborde, an archaeologist who was briefly in 1830 Prefect of the Seine (roughly the equivalent of Mayor of Paris), a title held a couple of decades later by the creator of ⑨ the **boulevard Haussmann**, one of the longest of the boulevards slashed through the city in the mid-19thC. The corner where the street and boulevard meet was an appropriate choice of site in 1989 for ⑩ **a statue of Baron Haussmann**, which had been languishing in the city art depository for half a century after its completion by Lon Cogné. ⑪ **Puiforcat** (131 boulevard Haussmann) specializes in silver, including copies of the superb pieces designed by Jean Puiforcat in the thirties, as well as the work of modern designers. ⑫ On fine summer days, the flower-filled courtyard/patio of **Le Marcande** (**FF-FFFF**, 52 rue de Miromesnil) makes a delightful setting for subtle and elegant cuisine.

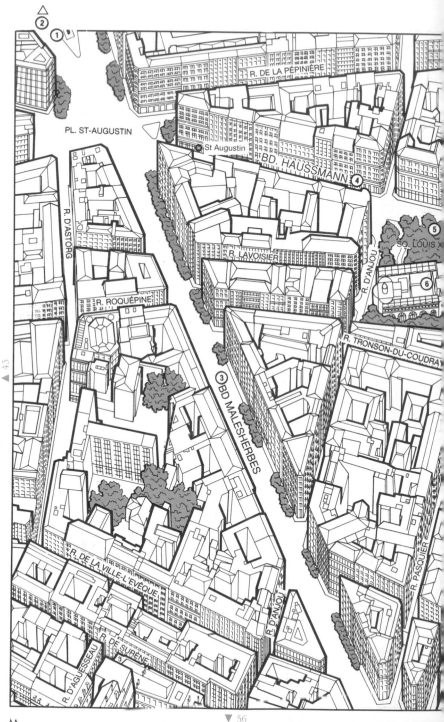

R. DE LA PÉPINIÈRE

PL. ST-AUGUSTIN

M St Augustin

BD. HAUSSMANN

R. D'ASTORG

R. LAVOISIER

SQ. LOUIS X

R. ROQUÉPINE

R. D'ANJOU

R. TRONSON-DU-COUDRA

BD MALESHERBES

R. DE LA VILLE-L'ÉVÊQUE

R. PASQUIER

R. D'ANJOU

DE SURÈNE

R. D'AGUESSEAU

▲ 45

▼ 56

Malesherbes

PL. GABRIEL-PÉRI

R. DE PROVENCE

R. PASQUIER

R. DE L'ARCADE

R. DE ROME

BD. HAUSSMANN

R. DES MATHURINS

R. GREFFULHE

R. DE CASTELLANE

R. D'ARCOLE

R. CHAUVEAU-LAGARDE

R. TRONCHET

S. DE LA DELEINE

① An **equestrian statue of Joan of Arc** by Paul Dubois, the great-nephew of the well-known sculptor Jean-Baptiste Pigalle, adorns the square in front of ② the **church of St-Augustin** (just off map), built by Victor Baltard, the architect of the late-lamented market pavilions at Les Halles (*see page 91*), on a wedge-shaped plan and an iron frame. Proust lived in both ③ the **boulevard Malesherbes** (no. 8) and ④ the **boulevard Haussmann** (no. 45, with the famous cork-lined room, and no. 102). ⑤ The **square Louis-XVI**, once the Cimetière de la Madeleine (Madeleine Cemetery), containing the graves of the Swiss Guards massacred at the Tuileries in 1792, and the 1300-odd men and women put to death on the guillotine, including Marie-Antoinette and Louis XVI, and Charlotte Corday. ⑥ The **Chapelle expiatoire** was built by Napoleon's favourite architects Percier and Fontaine for Louis XVIII, as a memorial to his guillotined brother and sister-in-law (whose remains had by then been removed to the royal basilica at St-Denis to the north of Paris). ⑦ The **Théâtre des Mathurins**, built in 1898, was the theatrical home of Ludmilla and Georges Pitoëff from 1937 to Georges's death in 1939; here they continued their policy of putting on plays by Ibsen and Chekhov, Pirandello, Shaw and Shakespeare. ⑧ In front of the Gare St-Lazare, an 'accumulation' of pieces of luggage by sculptor Arman, punningly entitled **Consigne à Vie** (a *consigne* is a left-luggage office), one of a pair commissioned by arts minister Jack Lang.

46

▼ 57

The Opéra

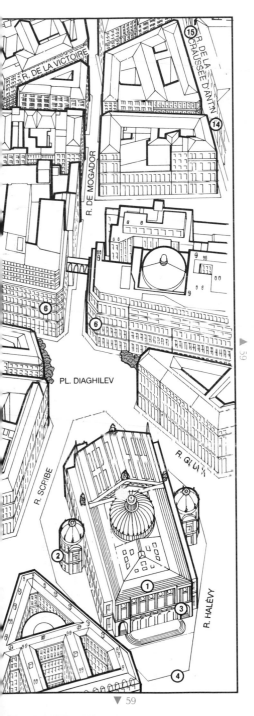

(1) The splendidly elaborate late 19thC **Opéra** (opera house), designed by a previously unknown architect, Charles Garnier, and famous for its grand marble staircase, its Grand Foyer decorated with paintings by Paul Baudry, its pretty Chagall ceiling – and its underground river, the source of many legends. (2) A **bust of Garnier** by Jean-Baptiste Carpeaux, who also carved (3) the graceful **La Danse** group on the Opéra's façade (both are copies). (4) The large square in front of the opera house was laid out by Baron Haussmann, whose eponymous boulevard (the **boulevard Haussmann**) is lined at this point by Paris's top department stores. (5) **Le Printemps** and (6) **Galeries Lafayette** are both particularly good for fashion, scents and accessories. (7) **Marks & Spencer**'s scones and Christmas puddings are a byword in the Anglophile community. (8) The **Lycée Condorcet**, in a fine neo-classical building by Alexandre-Théodore Brongniart (the architect of the Paris Bourse), originally a Capuchin monastery. (9) The monastery's chapel is now the **church of St-Louis d'Antin**. (10) The **passage du Havre**, a bustling shopping arcade, leads to (11) the **place du Havre** (just off map), fronting the monumental façade of (12) the **Gare St-Lazare** (off map), for trains to Normandy. (13) In the station forecourt (off map), a witty piece of sculpture by Arman, **L'Heure de tous** (1985), an 'accumulation' (the sculptor's term) of clocks. (14) Building work in the courtyard of a bank in the **rue de la Chaussée-d'Antin** in 1977 led to the surprise discovery of the missing heads of the Kings of Judah from the Galerie des Rois on the west front of Notre Dame, apparently buried there for safekeeping by a canny aristocrat during the French Revolution. (15) Joséphine de Beauharnais lived at **No. 62** during the period before her marriage to Napoleon. (16) **Poet riding Pegasus**, a monument to Victor Hugo by Alexandre Falguière, adorns (17) the **place de l'Opéra-Louis-Jouvet**, commemorating the great actor-director. (18) The round **place Edouard-VII**, a haven of peace in the busy, noisy Opéra district, centres on an equestrian statue of King Edward VII, son of Queen Victoria, in full dress uniform, by Paul Landowski. (19) Perfume enthusiasts should head for **L'Artisan parfumeur** (22 rue Vignon), specializing in natural fragrances, and cheese fiends for (20) **La Ferme St-Hubert** (No. 21), one of the city's top cheesemongers, with a small restaurant.

PL. AMIRAL-DE-GRASSE

PL. DES ETATS-UNIS

R. DE L'AMIRAL-D'ESTAING

R. HAMELIN

R. DE LÜBECK

AV. D'IÉNA

R. FREYCINET

PL. ROCHAMBEAU

R. BRIGNOLE

M Iéna

PL. D'IÉNA

AV. DU PRÉSIDENT-WILSON

Iéna M

AV. DU

AV. D'IÉNA

R. DE LA MANUTENTION

R. FRESNEL

R. FOUCAU

65

48

Iéna

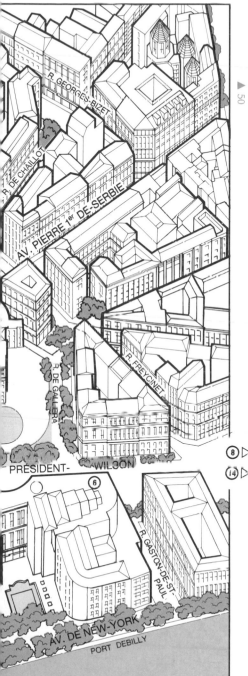

① The **place d'Iéna** commemorates the Battle of Jena of 1806, a major Napoleonic victory. ② It centres on an **equestrian statue of George Washington**, a gift from the Ladies of America in 1900. ③ An open-air food market is rather surprisingly held in the **avenue du Président Wilson**, best known for its museums. ④ The **Musée Guimet** specializes in Far Eastern art, while ⑤ the **Palais Galliéra**, an Italianate 19thC building with a pretty garden, houses the **Musée de la Mode et du Costume** (Fashion and Costume Museum, temporary exhibitions only). Opposite here, ⑥ the **Musée d'Art moderne de la Ville de Paris** (City of Paris Modern Art Museum, small cafeteria) has some interesting Matisses, and work by Picasso, Chagall, Modigliani and Rouault, among many other 20thC artists. ⑦ The other wing of the same building, the Palais de Tokyo, now houses the **Centre national de la Photographie**, staging popular temporary exhibitions on photography. ⑧ In and around the **place de l'Alma** (off map), several well-known restaurants: *Marius et Janette* (4 avenue George-V, **FFF**), an elegant fish restaurant, has spawned a less expensive annexe, the *Bistrot de Marius* (**F-FF**). ⑨ The **place des États-Unis**, in the heart of a posh residential district, boasts ⑩ a **statue of H.G. Wells** and ⑪ a symbol of Franco-American co-operation in the shape of a **statue of Lafayette and George Washington** solemnly shaking hands (off map), by the 19thC Alsace sculptor Frédéric-Auguste Bartholdi, the creator of New York's Statue of Liberty. ⑫ The **Goethe Institut** (17 avenue d'Iéna) stages lectures by and about German authors, concerts and debates. ⑬ The **Palais du Conseil économique et social** was designed in the late thirties by Auguste Perret, a specialist, with his brothers Claude and Gustave, in buildings with reinforced concrete frames; he is well known for ⑭ his **Théâtre des Champs-Elysées** in the avenue Montaigne (off map).

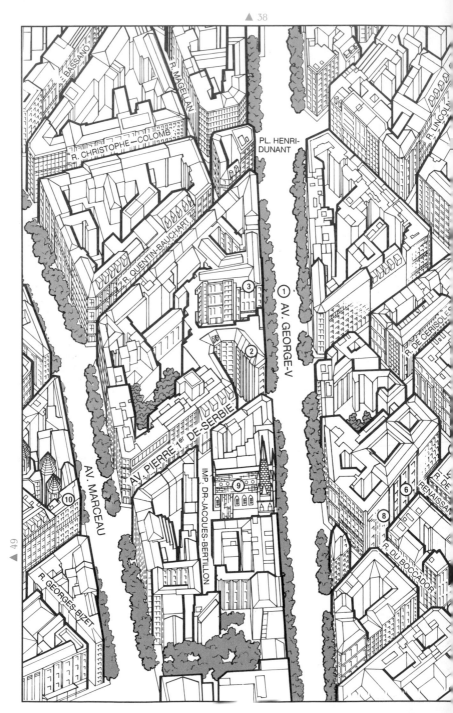

R. BASSANO

R. MAGELLAN

R. CHRISTOPHE—COLOMB

R. LINCOLN

PL. HENRI-DUNANT

2 R. QUENTIN-BAUCHART

③

① AV. GEORGE-V

②

R. DE CERISOLE

AV. PIERRE 1er DE-SERBIE

IMP. DR-JACQUES-BERTILLON

⑨

⑥

R. DE RENAISSANCE

⑧

AV. MARCEAU

⑩

R. DU BOCCADOR

▲ 49

R. GEORGES-BIZET

George-V

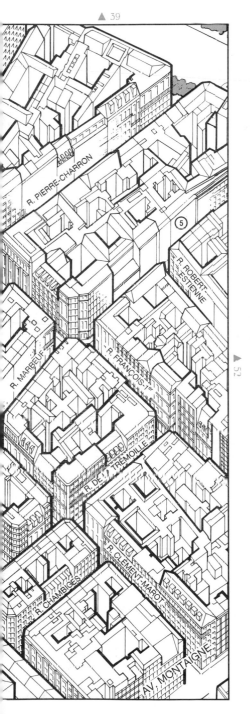

① The broad **avenue George-V**, named after Britain's monarch, is the heart of the plush eighth *arrondissement*, a byword for luxury hotels. ② The **George-V** (**FFFF**, 31 avenue George-V), a successful combination of old-world elegance and new-world functionalism, with an appropriately grand restaurant, *Les Princes*, and ③ the **Marriott-Prince de Galles** (**FFFF**, No. 33), another homage to a (future) British king, richly furnished with antiques and with some splendid thirties bathrooms, suitably updated, are just two of them; the latter's restaurant, called simply the *Prince de Galles*, a feast of art déco, surprisingly offers reasonably priced *menus* as well as the expensive *carte*. ④ Also very luxurious, but tucked away in a less busy street, **La Trémoïlle** (**FFFF**, 14 rue de la Trémoïlle). ⑤ The **rue Marbeuf** is a haven for gourmets only a few paces from the gastronomic desert of the Champs-Elysées. ⑥ At No. 15, Alsace restaurateur Guy-Pierre Baumann, famous for his inventive *choucroutes*, has decided to make a play on words involving the street name: **Baumann Marbeuf** (**FFF**) specializes in superb beef, including that summer favourite for Parisians, *steak tartare* (wide choice of seasonings), though it also serves excellent seafood. ⑦ **Chez André** at No. 12 (**FFF**) seems to have been going for ever: a genuine Paris bistrot only a stone's throw from the internationalized Champs-Elyses. ⑧ At No. 5, **La Fermette Marbeuf 1900** (**FF-FFF**) has a priceless asset in the shape of genuine art nouveau décor, so carefully concealed behind a fake wall that its discovery in the seventies was the pleasantest of surprises; good-value meals and a lively clientèle are two other plusses. ⑨ The American **Episcopal Cathedral of the Holy Trinity**, with a Gothic-style façade, dates from the 1880s, while ⑩ **St- Pierre de-Chaillot**, built half a century later, is neo-Romanesque.

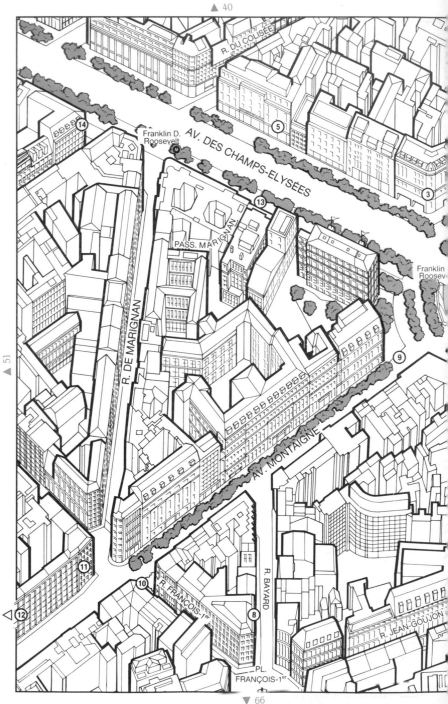

R. DU COLISÉE

⑤

③

Franklin D.
Roosevelt

AV. DES CHAMPS-ELYSÉES

⑭

⑬

PASS. MARIGNAN

Franklin
Roosev

R. DE MARIGNAN

⑨

AV. MONTAIGNE

⑪

R. BAYARD

⑩

R. FRANÇOIS-1er

⑧

⑫

R. JEAN-GOUJON

PL.
FRANÇOIS-1er

The Rond-Point

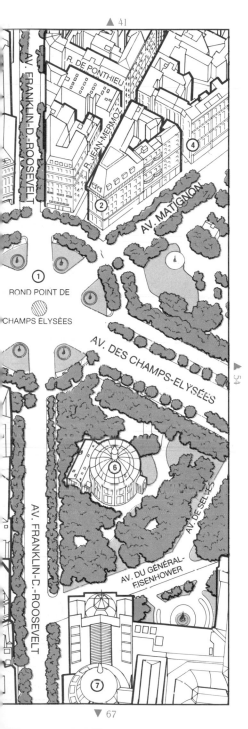

ROND POINT DE

CHAMPS ELYSÈES

▶ 54

① The **Rond-Point des Champs-Elysées**, a busy junction made attractive with flower-beds and fountains, is a good vantage poiont for admiring the views up the Champs-Elysées to the Arc de Triomphe (*see page 37*) and down to the place de la Concorde and the Tuileries Gardens (*see pages 72-3*). ② **Drugstore Publicis Matignon** (**FF**), a lively spot for a late-night meal or drink. ③ **Galerie Elysées-Rond-Point**, a modern arcade of luxury boutiques surrounding a peculiar structure designed to illustrate Leonardo's principle of perpetual motion. ④ **Artcurial**, a well-known modern art gallery, with a good art bookshop. ⑤ **Le Colisée**, a popular café for people-watching. ⑥ **Théâtre Renaud-Barrault**, once an ice rink where Colette used to skate, now the home of the company run by the great Jean-Louis Barrault and his wife Madeleine Renaud. The theatre has a pleasant restaurant (**FF**) open to non-theatregoers. ⑦ **Palais de la Découverte**, a rather didactic science museum with a very popular planetarium, in one wing of the Grand Palais (*see page 55*). ⑧ **The Scots Kirk** (7 rue Bayard). ⑨ **Avenue Montaigne**, once a lugubrious and bandit-infested path known as the *allée des Veuves* (Widows' Walk), was put on the map of fashionable Paris by 'Notre Dame de Thermidor', alias the Marquise de Fontenay, the lively wife of the Revolutionary leader Jean Lambert Tallien, who bought a house there and threw wild parties that attracted the bright young things of the time. It is now the respectable heart of couture land. ⑩ **Christian Dior** (No. 30). ⑪ **Nina Ricci** (No. 39). ⑫ **Guy Laroche** (No. 29) ⑬ **The Travellers' Club** (25 avenue des Champs-Elysées), housed in the only remaining mansion on the avenue, the Hôtel de la Païva, built by a famous Second Empire courtesan. ⑭ **L'Alsace** (No. 39, **FFF**), a lively brasserie serving filling Alsace dishes and excellent seafood 24 hours a day.

53

AV. MATIGNON

R. DU CIRQUE

① ◁
② ◁

③

AV. GABRIEL

④

AV. DE MARIGNY

⑥

⑤

Champs Élysées
Clemenceau
Ⓜ

PL. CLEMENCEAU

AV. DU GÉNÉRAL-EISENHOWER

⑪

⑫

AV. DES CHAMPS-ELYSÉES

⑩

AV. WINSTON-CHURCHILL

AV. CHARLES-GIRAULT

⑬

AV. DUTUIT

L'Elysée

► 56

①**Artcurial** (9 avenue Matignon, off map), a top Right Bank art gallery whose good bookshop has titles in several languages. ② The German poet Heinrich Heine died a couple of doors away at **No. 3** (off map), in February 1856. ③ The **Marché aux Timbres**, an open-air stamp and old postcard market, has long taken place on Thursdays and weekends between the avenue Matigny and the avenue de Marigny, beside ④ the circular **Théâtre Marigny**, built in 1881 by Charles Garnier, the architect of the Opéra (*see page 47*) to house a popular 'panorama'; it was converted into a music-hall with an open-air foyer, then, in the twenties, into a standard theatre. ⑤ The young Marcel Proust played in the **Jardin des Champs-Elysées** with Marie de Bernardaky, the model for Gilberte in *A la recherche du temps perdu*. ⑥ A **statue of Alphonse Daudet**, the Provençal author of *Lettres de mon moulin*, protected from the chill of white marble far from his sunny homeland by a travelling rug across his lap. ⑦ The **Palais de l'Elysée**, once the home of a string of beautiful women – Madame de Pompadour, Napoleon's sister Caroline Murat and his Empress Joséphine – has been the presidential palace since 1873. ⑧ Another of Napoleon's sisters, Pauline Borghese, lived in what is now the **British ambassador's residence** (39 rue du Faubourg St-Honoré), almost next door to ⑨ the **British Embassy** at No. 35, and, like the embassy and the Elysées Palace, enjoying private gardens stretching as far as the Champs-Elysées gardens (*see also page 57*). ⑩ The **Grand Palais**, built for the 1900 Exposition universelle (World's Exhibition), a massive stone and steel structure with a glass roof that looks quite magical lit up at night; the entrances on ⑪ the **avenue du Général-Eisenhower** and ⑫ the **place Clemenceau** lead to large galleries used for major art exhibitions, while ⑬ the much smaller **Petit Palais**, built at the same time, houses permanent collections ranging from 19thC French paintings to 18thC furniture, as well as staging temporary shows.

R. DE SURÈNE

BD MALESHERBES

R. D'AGUESSEAU

R. D'ANJOU

CITÉ DU RETIRO

CITÉ BERRYER

R. DU FAUBOURG-ST-HONORÉ

R. BOISSY-D'ANGLAS

R. ROYALE

Concorde

PL. DE LA CONCORDE

Madeleine

▲ 45

PL. DE LA MADELEINE

① Madeleine Ⓜ

② BD DE LA MADELEINE

R. RICHEPANSE

R. DUPHO...

R. ST-FLORENTIN

R. DU MONT-THABOR

R. DE MONDOVI

R. CAMBON

⑦

▶ 58

▼ 71

① The **church of Ste-Marie-Madeleine** (known to Parisians as 'la Madeleine'), built in the style of a classical temple, with an imposing Corinthian colonnade. ② Beside the church, an attractive open-air **flower market**. ③ and ④ **Fauchon**, probably the world's best-known grocer's, has mouthwatering window displays round the northeast corner of the place de la Madeleine, which is also home to ⑤ **Lucas-Carton**, with stunning Art Nouveau décor by Majorelle, still presided over by the brilliant chef-magician Alain Senderens, though it is now under Japanese ownership (**FFFF**, No. 9). ⑥ The **rue Royale** offers superb views across the place de la Concorde to the Palais Bourbon on the other side of the Seine (*see page 71*). ⑦ At No. 16, **Ladurée**, an elegant tea-room, whose well-heeled regulars no doubt buy their children adorable (and extremely expensive) outfits at ⑧ **Bonpoint** (No. 15). ⑨ Gold- and silversmiths **Christofle**, founded in 1830, now have their grand showrooms at No. 9, once the home of the philanthropist and connoisseur of applied art the Duc de la Rochefoucauld, a cousin of the Marquis de La Fayette (small musem). ⑩ The former town house of another duke, Armand-Emmanuel du Plessis, Duc de Richelieu, twice prime minister during the Restoration, houses the celebrated **Maxim's**, a landmark now owned by couturier Pierre Cardin and still boasting the turn-of-the-century décor of its heyday as the restaurant frequented by *le tout Paris* (No. 3, **FFFF**). ⑪ Madame de Staël lived at **No. 6** at the end of her life, with her second husband who was a good twenty years younger. ⑫ The elegant **rue du Faubourg St-Honoré**, lined with luxury fashion boutiques and *parfumiers*. ⑬ **Hermès** (No. 24) must be the best-known saddler's in the world, and still sells fabulous hand-stitched leather goods, as well as its famous silk headscarves. ⑭ The **Cercle Interallié** (No. 33), a top people's club, with swimming-pool and restaurant, in an early 18thC mansion. ⑮ The **British Embassy** next door, dating from less than a decade later, was the home in the early 19thC of Pauline Borghese, one of Napoleon's sisters, who sold it to the Duke of Wellington. ⑯ The **American Embassy** (2 avenue Gabriel), a few paces away from ⑰ the deluxe **Hôtel Crillon**, in a grand mansion designed by Gabriel, whose twin houses ⑱ the **Ministère de la Marine** (Navy Ministry).

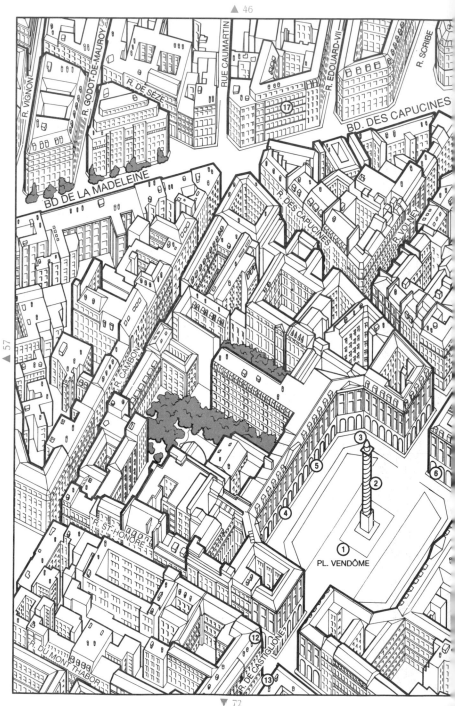

Place Vendôme

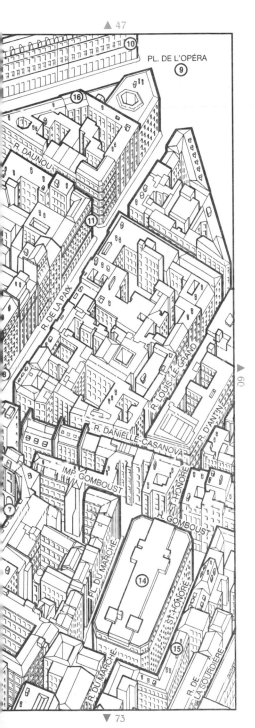

PL. DE L'OPÉRA

① The place **Vendôme**, surrounded by elegant 17thC buildings designed by Jules Hardouin-Mansart, is dominated by ② the lofty **Colonne Vendôme**, modelled on Trajan's Column in Rome and covered with episodes from the Battle of Austerlitz carved in bronze melted down from enemy cannons captured during the fighting. ③ Perched on top, a **statue of Napoleon in Roman dress**. Beside ④ the **Ministry of Justice**, ⑤ the **Ritz Hotel**, still very grand despite recent modernization, with a famous bar and *L'Espadon*, a luxury restaurant (**FFFF**, classical cuisine). ⑥ Ever since the days of Csar Ritz, the hotel's guests have also patronized **Boucheron** (No. 26) and ⑦ **Van Cleef et Arpels** (No. 22), two of the top jewellers in and around the square. ⑧ **Cartier** is just round the corner in the rue de la Paix, which leads to ⑨ the **place de l'Opéra**, a Haussmann creation fronting the majestic opera house (*see page 47*). ⑩ The long-fashionable **Café de la Paix**, its restaurant ceiling designed by the Opéra's architect Charles Garnier. ⑪ **Harry's Bar**, a mecca for visiting Americans. ⑫ **Godiva** (237 rue St-Honoré), for superlative Belgian chocolates. ⑬ **Le Carré des Feuillants** (14 rue de Castiglione, **FFFF**), excellent cuisine with a southwest flavour. *Feuillants* comes from the strict Bernardines whose monastery was once here, close to that of the *Jacobins* (Dominican friars) in what is now ⑭ the **place du Marché St-Honoré**, housing a covered market and several lively restaurants. ⑮ **L'Absinthe** (No. 24, **FFF**), chic yet relaxed, newish cuisine. ⑯ The first Impressionist exhibition was held, to much hostile criticism, in the studio rented by the great photographer Nadar at **35 boulevard des Capucines**. ⑰ The **Olympia** music hall, still a top showbiz venue. Piaf, Montand *et al* regularly drew the crowds here

Bibliothèque nationale

① **Drouant** (18 rue Gaillon, **FFF**) offers excellent, mainly classical, cuisine but its worldwide reputation comes from the annual gathering in one of its private dining rooms at which the winner of the Prix Goncourt, Europe's best-known book prize, is chosen, to enormous media fanfare. ② The **Fontaine Gaillon**, rebuilt in the 1820s by Louis Visconti, the architect of Napoleon's Tomb (*see page 97*), features a triton astride a dolphin. ③ Alexandre Dumas *fils*, author of *The Lady of the Camélias* and the illegitimate son of the creator of *The Three Musketeers*, was born in his twenty-two-year-old father's house in the **place Boïeldieu**, right opposite ④ the **Opéra Comique**, the home of light opera and operetta. This elaborate 19thC theatre is on the site of the Théatre des Italiens, the grand mansion where the Duc de Choiseul played host to the Italian troupe of actors who are commemorated in ⑤ the nearby **boulevard des Italiens** (off map), one of the legendary 'Grands Boulevards' of which Yves Montand sings so fetchingly. ⑥ The **Hôtel Favart** (5 rue Marivaux, **FF**) makes a quiet base in this busy central district. ⑦ The **rue des Colonnes**, an unexpected sight with its heavy columns supporting an arcade, built right at the end of the 18thC as a covered passage-way. ⑧ Gustave Eiffel, of Eiffel Tower fame, designed the iron frame of the huge **Crédit Lyonnais** bank. ⑨ Jacques Offenbach, the inventor of modern *opéra bouffe*, was the manager from 1855 of the **Bouffes parisiens** theatre, where his *Orpheus in the Underworld* was first performed; it now puts on straight plays. ⑩ The **square Louvois**, on the site of the theatre where, in 1820, the Duc de Berry was assassinated during a performance by a fanatic bent on wiping out the Bourbon dynasty. ⑪ Sculptures personifying four French rivers grace the charming **Fontaine Louvois**, another design by Visconti. ⑫ Opposite the fountain, the main entrance to the **Bilbiothèque nationale**, France's premier copyright library, whose books will move in the mid-nineties to a futuristic new building beside the Seine; temporary exhibitions are held in the beautiful Galerie Mazarine and the Cabinet des Médailles et Antiques has a permanent display of coins, medals and cameos. ⑬ The **rue Sainte-Anne** is famous for its gay clubs.

Bourse

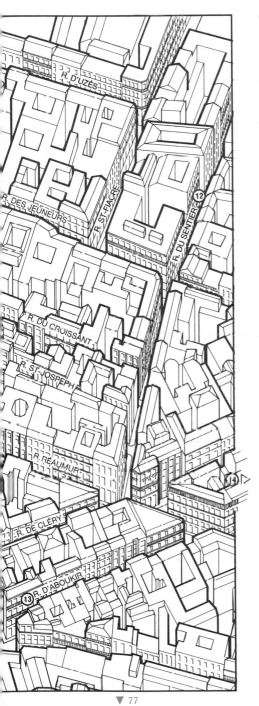

① The **Passage des Panoramas**, a glass-roofed 19thC shopping arcade lined with tiny shops, restaurants and tearooms, where Robert Fulton, an American, displayed his revolving 'panoramas' to a delighted audience, who later rejoiced in Offenbach's *La Belle Hélène* at ② the **Théâtre des Variétés** (off map), whose stage door opens into ③ the **Galerie des Variétés**, intersecting with the Passage des Panoramas and with the same fake marble decoration. ④ Another major attraction, still open today, the **Musée Grévin** (off map), Paris's waxworks, opened in 1882 by the cartoonist and draughtsman Alfred Grévin (10 boulevard Montmartre, off map). ⑤ The museum's window displays can be seen in the **Passage Jouffroy** (off map), the continuation, on the other side of the boulevard Montmartre, of the Passage des Panoramas. ⑥ At No. 34, **Galerie 34**, a tiny shop specializing in antique walking sticks and canes. ⑦ The **rue Brongniart** commemorates the 18thC architect of ⑧ the **Palais de la Bourse** (Paris stock exchange, guided tours weekday mornings). ⑨ The financial upper crust take time off for lunch at the small and elegant **Pile ou Face** (52bis rue Notre-Dame-des-Victoires, **FFFF**), while their more lowly brethren, and a lively crowd of late-night diners, flock to ⑩ **Le Vaudeville** (29 rue Vivienne, **FFF**) for a brasserie-type meal in a genuine thirties setting, or to ⑪ the cosy **Gallopin** (40 rue Notre-Dame-des-Vic toires, **FFF**), all mahogany and brass. ⑫ The **rue du Sentier**, the high street of Paris's rag trade district, known as 'Le Sentier'. ⑬ The **rue d'Aboukir**, one of a cluster of streets renamed to celebrate Napoleon's victories in Egypt. The Egyptomania of the time is epitomized in the entrance to ⑭ the **passage du Caire** (off map), adorned with huge pharoah's heads. ⑮ The **church of Notre-Dame-des-Victoires**, started in 1629, but not completed for over a century, also commemorates French glory won in battle, this time under Louis XIII, who features in a paintings by Van Loo inside the church, a pilgrimage centre since the early 19thC and covered with tens of thousands of *ex voto*. ⑯ Among many illustrious inhabitants of the **rue du Mail**, Franz Liszt lived at No. 13 for over half a century from 1823.

▼ 77

AV. RAYMOND-POINCARE

AV. KLÉBER

R. DE MAGDEBOU

AV. D'EYLAU

PL. DU
TROCADÉRO ET DU
ONZE-NOVEMBRE

Trocadéro

R. FRANKLIN

AV. ALBERT-1ᵉʳ-DE-MONACO

JARDINS DU PALAIS DE CHAILLOT

PL. DE VARSOVIE

① The **place du Trocadéro**, in the heart of the upmarket residential sixteenth *arrondissement*, commemorates the French storming of a fortress of the same name in the Bay of Cadiz in 1823. ② One of six avenues radiating from the square, the **avenue Kléber** is named after a Napoleonic general who was assassinated by a Turkish fanatic in Cairo in 1800, while the square is adorned with ③ a **statue of Marshal Foch**, another top military man, born in 1851. ④ The curving east wing of the **Palais de Chaillot**, built for the World's Exhibition of 1937, houses the **Théâtre national de Chaillot**, the latest incarnation of the great Jean Vilar's Théâtre national populaire, the **Musée de l'Homme** (Anthropology Museum) and the **Musée de la Marine** (Maritime Museum), plus a restaurant. ⑤ The **Musée des Monuments français** (Comparative Sculpture Museum) takes up a large part of the west wing, which has a magical **Musée du Cinéma** (Cinema Museum) in the basement, alongside one of Paris's two cinémathèques. ⑥ On the **Esplanade** between the two wings (impressive views of the Eiffel Tower), a row of gilded statues, including a *Flora* by Marcel Gimond, stands guard. ⑦ The **Jardins du Palais de Chaillot**, centring on an elongated ornamental pool, enlivened by fountains and surrounded by groups of statuary. ⑧ The **rue Franklin** leads to the chic Passy district. ⑨ At No. 8, the little **Musée Clemenceau** (off map), devoted to the left-wing French statesman Georges Clemenceau, nicknamed 'The Tiger'. ⑩ The **Brasserie Le Coq** (2 place du Trocadéro, **FF**), one of several chic restaurants and café/tea-rooms with strategic pavement terraces.

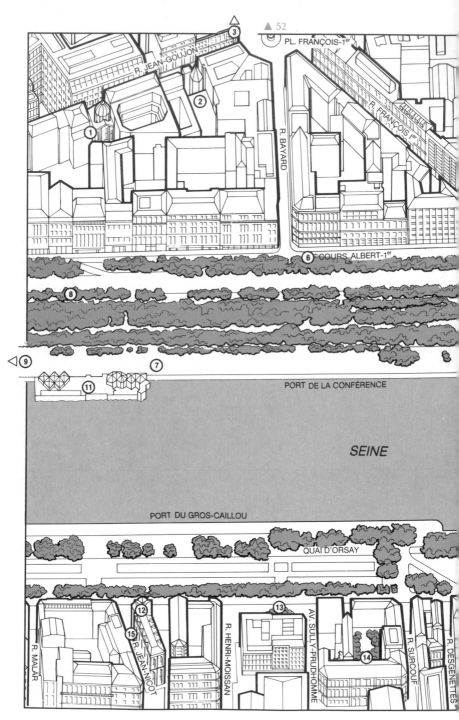

▲ 52
PL. FRANÇOIS-1er

R. JEAN-GOUJON

R. FRANÇOIS 1er

R. BAYARD

6 COURS ALBERT-1er

8

9

7

PORT DE LA CONFÉRENCE

11

SEINE

PORT DU GROS-CAILLOU

QUAI D'ORSAY

12

13

15

R. JEAN-NICOT

R. HENRI-MOISSAN

AV. SULLY-PRUDHOMME

14

R. SURCOUF

R. DESGENETTES

R. MALAR

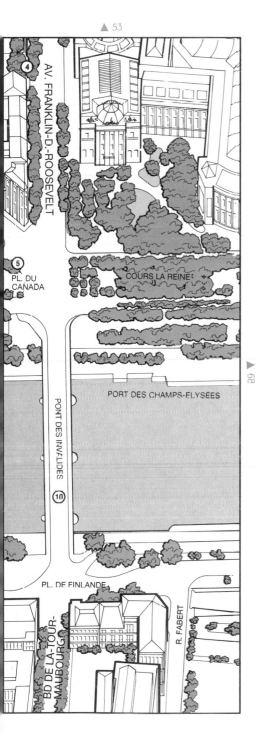

François 1er/Quai d'Orsay

① **Notre-Dame de Consolation**, a church built in 1901 to commemorate the victims of a famous fire four years earlier during an aristocratic fund-raising event, the Bazar de la Charit, held in a wooden structure on this spot. The press was quick to point out that although the 1500-strong crowd included as many elegantly garbed gentlemen as duchesses and baronesses, all but five of the 125 who died were women – many of them trampled underfoot by their fleeing escorts. ② The **Chapelle arménienne** (Armenian Chapel) dates from 1903. ③ The patrons of the charming and luxurious **Hôtel San Régis** (**FFFF**, 12 rue Jean-Goujon) can no doubt afford to eat in ④ **Lasserre** (**FFFF**), one of the city's best-known luxury restaurants, in an attractive town house dwarfed by undistinguished buildings. ⑤ The **place du Canada**, planned as a convenient turning place for carriages parading along Queen Marie de Médicis's version of an Italian *corso*, the Cours-la-Reine, whose western half was renamed in 1918 ⑥ the **Cours Albert 1er** to honour the Belgian king Albert I. ⑦ The high-level discussions commemorated by the **quai de la Conférence** took place in 1660 and were attended by Spanish envoys who processed through the now-vanished 'Conference Gateway' near here to meet Cardinal Mazarin to discuss a potential marriage between Louis XIV and the Infanta Maria Theresa. ⑧ The **monument to Adam Mickiewicz**, commissioned from Antoine Bourdelle by the Polish government as a gift to the people of Paris, depicts the Polish poet and patriot as a pilgrim striding resolutely forwards, staff in hand. ⑨ When the **Pont de l'Alma** (off map) was rebuilt in the early seventies, only one of the four statues was retained. This statue, the Zouave, representing a regiment which fought at the Battle of Alma in the Crimea, is popular with Parisians as a handy way of checking the height of the Seine (in 1910 the rising waters famously tickled his chin). Between the bridge and ⑩ the **Pont des Invalides**, built in the 1820s, ⑪ the **landing stage for the Bateaux-Mouches** sightseeing boats. ⑫ the **American Church in Paris**, a few doors away from ⑬ the modern building of the **South African Embassy**. ⑭ The **Seita**, the headquarters of the State tobacco authority, on the site of a large tobacco factory; the **Musée de la Seita** (12 rue Surcouf) is devoted to the history of tobacco, introduced into France by the 16thC diplomat, appropriately honoured in ⑮ the nearby **rue Jean-Nicot**, who gave his name to nicotine.

AV. FRANKLIN-D.-ROOSEVELT

④

⑤
PL. DU CANADA

COURS LA REINE

PORT DES CHAMPS-ÉLYSÉES

PONT DES INVALIDES

⑩

PL. DE FINLANDE

BD DE LA-TOUR-MAUBOURG

R. FABERT

68 ▶

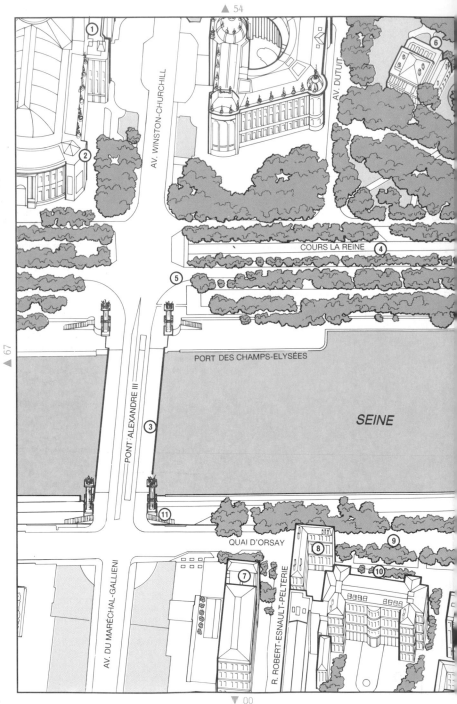

AV. WINSTON-CHURCHILL

AV. DUTUIT

COURS LA REINE

PONT ALEXANDRE III

PORT DES CHAMPS-ELYSÉES

SEINE

QUAI D'ORSAY

AV. DU MARÉCHAL-GALLIENI

R. ROBERT-ESNAULT-PELTERIE

Cours la Reine/Quai d'Orsay

① The southern half of the **Grand Palais** is used for prestige trade fairs and art shows, and for one of Paris's newly anonymous universities, Paris IV. ② The superb **flying chariot-and-four** on the south-east corner is by a curiously little-known sculptor, Georges Recipon, who also designed and cast the beaten copper groups on the centre of ③ the **Pont Alexandre III**, undoubtedly Paris's prettiest bridge, adorned with cupids and twirling lamps. ④ The tree-lined **Cours-la-Reine**, named after Queen Marie de Médicis, who planned it as the fashionable promenade it soon became. ⑤ An equestrian **statue of Simón Bolívar** by Emmanuel Frémiet, the sculptor who cast the standard-bearing Joan of Arc in the place des Pyramides (*see page 73*). The original was commissioned by the Colombian government; this is a copy presented to the City of Paris on the centenary of the death of South America's 'Liberator' by the Spanish-speaking nations of Bolivia, Colombia, Ecuador, Panama, Peru and Venezuela. ⑥ The deluxe **Restaurant Ledoyen** (**FFFF**) started life as a modest wooden shack, selling refreshments to customers 'At the Sign of the Dolphin'. ⑦ The **Gare des Invalides**, a busy station on the C line of the RER (trains travel westwards from here to Versailles). ⑧ The **Ministère des Relations extérieures** (Foreign Ministry) is usually referred to by the name of the embankment running beside the Seine, ⑨ the **Quai d'Orsay**. ⑩ Standing proudly in front of the ministry, a **statue of Aristide Briand**, who was appointed foreign minister no fewer than fifteen times. A great parliamentary orator nicknamed the 'Pilgrim of Peace' (he won the Nobel Peace Prize in 1926), he was also eleven times President of the Council (prime minister). At the Left Bank (southern) end of the Pont Alexandre III, ⑪ a stone group at the foot of one of the slender towers, by Laurent Marqueste, a sulptor from Toulouse, depicts **The France of Louis XIV**.

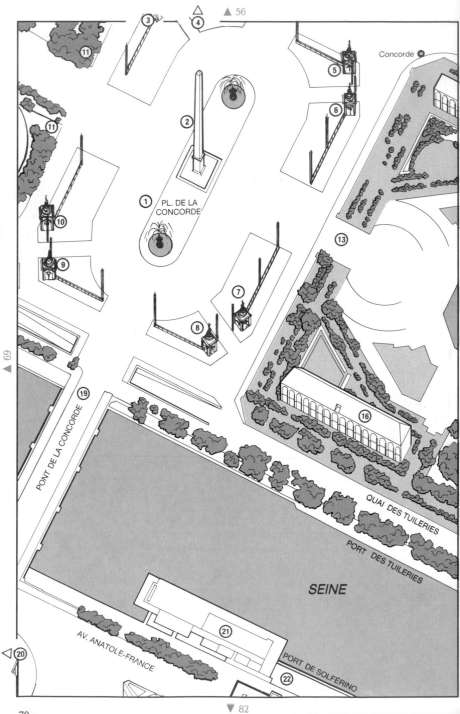

▲ 69

PL. DE LA CONCORDE

Concorde Ⓜ

PONT DE LA CONCORDE

QUAI DES TUILERIES

PORT DES TUILERIES

SEINE

AV. ANATOLE-FRANCE

PORT DE SOLFÉRINO

Concorde

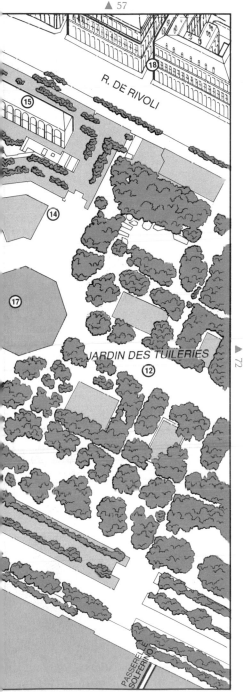

▶ 72

① The vast **place de la Concorde**, laid out in the mid-18thC by Jacques-Ange Gabriel as the **place Louis XV** (it originally centred on a statue of 'Louis the Beloved' as he was known). Constantly snarled up with traffic, it is still beautiful, offering majestic vistas in all four directions. ② In the centre now, a granite **Obelisk from Luxor**, dating back to Rameses III (1198-67 BC). It was presented by Egypt to the people of France and chosen by Louis-Philippe as a safely uncontroversial alternative to some royal personage. The oval main square is adorned with a series of allegorical figures symbolizing eight major French towns: ③ **Brest**, ④ **Rouen**, ⑤ **Lille**, ⑥ **Strasbourg** (for which the actress Juliette Drouet, faithful mistress to Victor Hugo for half a century, posed), ⑦ **Lyon**, ⑧ **Marseille**, ⑨ **Bordeaux** and ⑩ **Nantes**. Juliette Drouet had previously been the mistress of James Pradier, who sculpted the figures of Lille and Strasbourg; the others – two each – are by lesser artists: Caillouette, Cortot and Petitot. ⑪ The **Chevaux de Marly**, a pair of rearing horses by Guillaume Cousteau, originally on the huge drinking trough fronting the royal chteau of Marly, west of Paris. Facing them, at the entrance to ⑫ the **Tuileries Gardens**, are ⑬ another brace of horses, this time **winged steeds** ridden by Fame and Mercury. They are by Cousteau's uncle Antoine Coysevox, who also carved ⑭ **a bust of the royal gardener André Le Nôtre** (a copy of one in St-Roch). ⑮ The **Jeu de Paume** housed until the mid-80s Paris's famous Impressionists, now in the Musée d'Orsay (*see page 83*). Now refurbished, it is being used for temporary art exhibitions. ⑯ **L'Orangerie** has a good collection of late 19thC and early 20thC painting, plus a roomful of glorious Monet *Waterlilies*. ⑰ Sailing boats in the **Bassin des Tuileries** is a favourite Parisian pastime, as popular with grown-up small boys as with the genuine article. ⑱ Smith & Son's **English Bookshop** has been in business since 1903 (its English Tea Rooms are, alas, no more, recently sacrificed to a new floor of books). ⑲ The **Pont de la Concorde**, a good place for appreciating the traditional French predilection for symmetry: to the south, echoing the classical façade of the church of the Madeleine (*see page 57*), ⑳ the imposing **Palais Bourbon**, home of France's Parliament (the Assemblée Nationale) since the Restoration. ㉑ The **Piscine Deligny**, a popular floating swimming-pool (topless sunbathing virtually *de rigueur*). ㉒ **The landing stage for the barge cruises** to the Parc de la Villette (*see pages 19, 29*).

71

R. ROUGET-DE-L'ISLE

①

⑪

R. ST-HONORÉ

⑬

R. DE CASTIGLIONE

R. DU MONT-THABOR

⑫

R. D'ALGER

⑭ ⑮

R. DU 29 JUILL

⑩

R. DE RIVOLI ⑨

②

JARDIN DES TUILERIES

③

Tuileries

① The **rue Rouget-de-Lisle** commemorates the army captain who in 1792 wrote the battle hymn that was to become France's stirring national anthem, *La Marseillaise*. ② The **Jardin des Tuileries**, formal gardens in the French manner designed by Louis XIV's master gardener André Le Nôtre as the first stage in a long 'triumphal way' sweeping westwards from the Louvre Palace to St-Germain-en-Laye. ③ The eastern end of the gardens is dotted with **bronzes of plump female nudes** by Aristide Maillol. They will eventually move back to their original setting (decreed by General de Gaulle's arts minister André Malraux) in ④ the **Jardin du Carrousel**, due for redesigning and replanting as part of the 'Grand Louvre' project. ⑤ The **Pavillon de Marsan**, all that is left of Catherine de Médicis's Tuileries Palace (and almost entirely rebuilt). ⑥ Its upper storeys have been stylishly fitted out as the **Musée des Arts de la Mode** (Fashion Arts Museum, entrance 109 rue de Rivoli), displaying costumes and couture outfits and accessories from ⑦ the **Musée des Arts décoratifs** (Applied and Decorative Arts Museum), its exhibits now reorganized, with a greater emphasis on the 20thC, including a new 'Contemporary Gallery' of postwar designer pieces (bookshop, classy gift boutique). ⑧ A brilliantly regilded equestrian **statue of Joan of Arc** in full armour, by Emmanuel Frémiet, nephew of François Rude, whose own sculpture of the Maid of Orléans is now in the Louvre. ⑨ Napoleon named the elegant arcaded **rue de Rivoli**, built in 1802, after a battle in which his armies scored a victory over the Austrians five years earlier. A wall running along ⑩ the **Terrasse des Feuillants** formed an enclosure for the monastery buildings inhabited by a community of Feuillants (strict Bernardines), who are also commemorated in ⑪ **Le Carré des Feuillants** (14 rue de Castiglione, **FFF-FFFF**), top restaurant with a south-western flavour. ⑫ Alfred de Musset spent his last few years at **6 rue du Mont-Thabor**, dying there in 1857 of 'the poisoned embrace of the green muse', as Alexandre Dumas poetically described an addiction to absinthe. ⑬ The deluxe **Hôtel Intercontinental (FFFF)**, popular for its open-air patio with tinkling fountain. ⑭ The restaurant once on the site of the equally deluxe **Hôtel Meurice** (the Nazi commandant's wartime HQ) staged a special celebration for Robespierre and Saint-Just the day after Marie-Antoinette's death on the guillotine. ⑮ **Galignani** (No. 224), old-established Anglo-French bookshop. ⑯ The Baroque **Saint-Roch**, where both royal gardener Le Nôtre and classical dramatist Pierre Corneille are buried.

Palais Royal

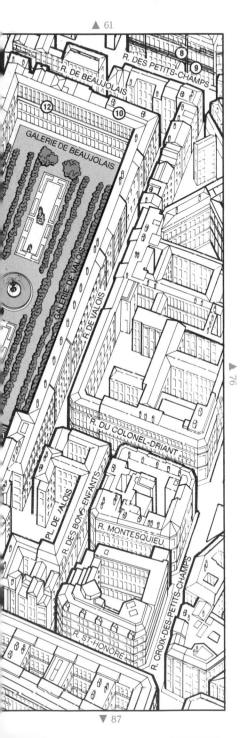

① **Normandy Hôtel** (7 rue de l'Echelle, **FFF**), old-established hotel with a popular bar in what the French refer to as 'English club' style. ② In the twenties, **No. 5** in the same street was one of Paris's most fashionable restaurants, run by brilliant chef Prosper Montagné. ③ The **rue Molière** leading to ④ the **rue Richelieu** where, on the site of No. 40, the great comic playwright died on 16 February 1673, after collapsing on stage at ⑤ the **Théâtre français**, better known outside France as the **Comédie française**. The theatre's mirror-lined upstairs gallery displays the armchair in which he was sitting, during a performance of his play *Le Malade imaginaire*, when the fatal incident happened, exactly as depicted on ⑥ the **Fontaine Molière**. ⑦ **Au Bec fin** (6 rue Thérèse), one of Paris's dwindling band of *cafés-théâtres*. ⑧ **Le Grand Colbert** (passage Colbert, **FF**), a new brasserie in traditional Central European style, with newspapers mounted on long sticks, in an arcade (off map) that also houses ⑨ a little shop selling cards and prints reproducing items from the nearby Bibliothèque nationale (*see page 61*). ⑩ The novelist Colette lived at **9 rue de Beaujolais**, her drawing-room windows overlooking ⑪ the **Jardin du Palais-Royal**, a tree-lined oasis of peace in the heart of the city (though in the 18thC and 19thC it was notorious for its gambling dens). Both she and her neighbour Jean Cocteau were habitués of ⑫ the beautiful and long-famous restaurant **Le Grand Véfour** (17 rue de Beaujolais, **FFFF**). The grand reception rooms of ⑬ the **Ministère de la Culture et de la Communication** (arts and media ministry) appropriately overlook ⑭ one of the most controversial 'monuments' commissioned by President Mitterrand's flamboyant arts minister Jack Lang, the **Colonnes de Buren**, a mini-landscape of striped columns in black-and-white marble, some short, some tall, created by sculptor Daniel Buren. ⑮ Part of what was originally the palatial residence of Cardinal Richelieu, who left it to his royal master Louis XIII in his will – hence the name 'Royal Palace' – now houses the **Conseil d'Etat** (Council of State), a top administrative body whose very senior civil servants form an unofficial but highly influential political club. ⑯ On the opposite side of the square, the **passage Richelieu** offers a superb view of the Louvre Pyramid (*see pages 86-7*). ⑰ The **Aile Richelieu** (Richelieu Wing) of the Louvre, housing the Ministre des Finances (Finance Ministry) until it was moved to a brand-new riverside site in 1989, is due to open in 1993 as new painting galleries. ⑱ The **Louvre des Antiquaires**, an antiques emporium.

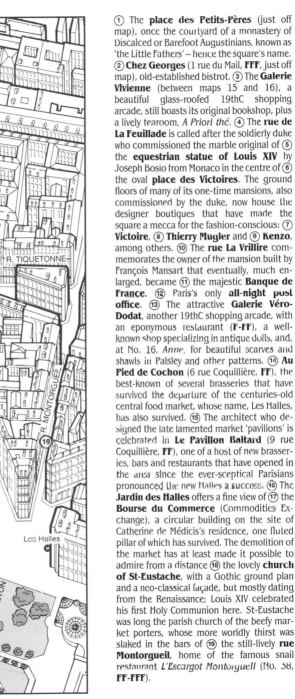

① The **place des Petits-Pères** (just off map), once the courtyard of a monastery of Discalced or Barefoot Augustinians, known as 'the Little Fathers' – hence the square's name. ② **Chez Georges** (1 rue du Mail, **FFF**, just off map), old-established bistrot. ③ The **Galerie Vivienne** (between maps 15 and 16), a beautiful glass-roofed 19thC shopping arcade, still boasts its original bookshop, plus a lively tearoom, A Priori thé. ④ The **rue de La Feuillade** is called after the soldierly duke who commissioned the marble original of ⑤ the **equestrian statue of Louis XIV** by Joseph Bosio from Monaco in the centre of ⑥ the oval **place des Victoires**. The ground floors of many of its one-time mansions, also commissioned by the duke, now house the designer boutiques that have made the square a mecca for the fashion-conscious: ⑦ **Victoire**, ⑧ **Thierry Mugler** and ⑨ **Kenzo**, among others. ⑩ The **rue La Vrillire** commemorates the owner of the mansion built by François Mansart that eventually, much enlarged, became ⑪ the majestic **Banque de France**. ⑫ Paris's only **all-night post office**. ⑬ The attractive **Galerie Véro-Dodat**, another 19thC shopping arcade, with an eponymous restaurant (**F-FF**), a well-known shop specializing in antique dolls, and, at No. 16, Anne, for beautiful scarves and shawls in Paisley and other patterns. ⑭ **Au Pied de Cochon** (6 rue Coquillière, **FF**), the best-known of several brasseries that have survived the departure of the centuries-old central food market, whose name, Les Halles, has also survived. ⑮ The architect who designed the late lamented market 'pavilions' is celebrated in **Le Pavillon Baltard** (9 rue Coquillière, **FF**), one of a host of new brasseries, bars and restaurants that have opened in the area since the ever-sceptical Parisians pronounced the new Halles a success. ⑯ The **Jardin des Halles** offers a fine view of ⑰ the **Bourse du Commerce** (Commodities Exchange), a circular building on the site of Catherine de Médicis's residence, one fluted pillar of which has survived. The demolition of the market has at least made it possible to admire from a distance ⑱ the lovely **church of St-Eustache**, with a Gothic ground plan and a neo-classical façade, but mostly dating from the Renaissance; Louis XIV celebrated his first Holy Communion here. St-Eustache was long the parish church of the beefy market porters, whose more worldly thirst was slaked in the bars of ⑲ the still-lively **rue Montorgueil**, home of the famous snail restaurant L'Escargot Montorgueil (No. 38, **FF-FFF**).

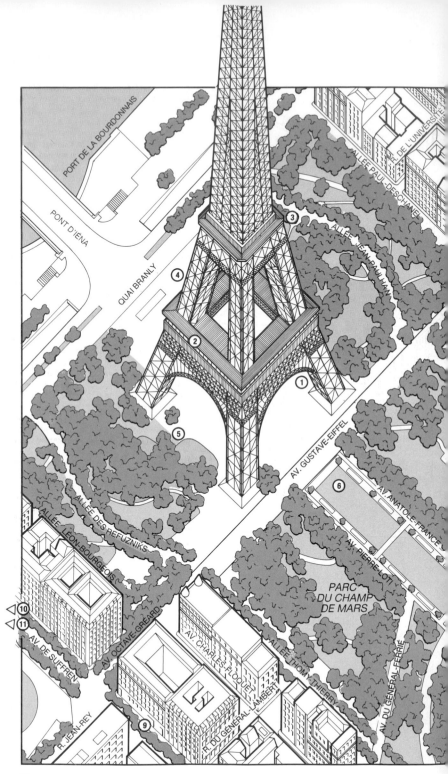

Eiffel Tower

① The **Eiffel Tower**, familiar from a thousand kitsch souvenirs and, at over 300 metres/nearly 1000 ft tall, visible from all over Paris, was built for the World's Exhibition of 1889. Planned as a temporary memorial to commemorate the centenary of the French Revolution, derided by artists and writers, it was a popular favourite from the start, and pulling it down soon became unthinkable. ② The **first floor** has a small museum on the tower's history, with video presentation, post office and boutiques. ③ Continue to the second floor and you can dine in style at the **Jules Verne (FFF-FFFF**, book well in advance), with Paris at your feet. ④ A **bust of Gustave Eiffel** by Antoine Bourdelle, near the Pilier nord (north strut). ⑤ A romantic **artificial grotto** nestles between the south and west struts. While the tower end of ⑥ the **Champ de Mars**, originally a parade ground for cadets from ⑦ the **Ecole militaire** (military academy, off map), designed in the mid-18thC by Jacques-Ange Gabriel, is now an informal *jardin à l'anglaise*, the other end is a neat and formal *jardin à la française*. ⑧ The old-established **Guignol** (Punch & Judy theatre, just off map) vies in popularity with pony rides up and down the gravelly paths between the fenced-off flowerbeds and strips of lawn. ⑨ The **avenue de Suffren** (off map), lined with elegant blocks of spacious bourgeois flats. ⑩ The **Hilton International Paris (FFFF**, entrance 18 avenue de Suffren), the city's first huge modern hotel, on the edge of the high-rise 'Front de Seine' district beside the river. ⑪ Further down the avenue (off map) the **Village suisse**, a little enclave of antique shops. ⑫ The **square Rapp** (off map), a feast for art nouveau lovers, with buildings by Jules Lavirotte, who also designed the exuberant façade of ⑬ **No. 29 avenue Rapp** (off map). ⑭ At the river end of the avenue Rapp, the entrance to **Les Egouts** (off map), Paris's famous (and famously creepy) sewers.

R. DE L'UNIVERSITÉ

⑧

Invalides (R.E.R.) Ⓜ

AV. DU MARECHAL-GALLIENI

R. DE CONSTANTINE

④
⑤
⑥

⑫

③

① *ESPLANADE DES INVALIDES*

R. DE TALLEYRAND

R. DE GRENELLE

②
PL. DES INVALIDES

BD DES INVALIDES

▶ 32

Faubourg Saint-Germain/Invalides

① The **Esplanade des Invalides**, laid out in the early 18thC by Robert de Cotte, the brother-in-law and pupil of Jules Hardouin-Mansart, the architect of the Hôtel des Invalides (*see pages 96-7*), whom he succeeded as premier architecte du roi. ② Overlooking the **place des Invalides**, a battery of bronze guns guards the entrance to the formal garden fronting Les Invalides. In ③ the **rue de Constantine**, a little enclave of English-language cultural promotion formed by ④ the **Canadian Cultural Centre** (No. 5), ⑤ the **British Council**'s Paris offices, including a good library (annual subscription), adjoining ⑥ the **British Institute** (Nos 9-11). ⑦ The **Invalides Air Terminal**, for Air France coaches serving Orly Airport, with a good restaurant, **Chez Françoise (FF-FFF)**, popular with officials from the Foreign Ministry a few steps away. ⑧ The **rue de l'Université**, stretching eastwards to St-Germain-des-Prés and lined with aristocratic mansions, many of them now ministries. ⑨ The late 18thC **place du Palais-Bourbon**, whose calm elegance is frequently shattered by grand official cars, escorted by well-armed motorcycle police, driving into the courtyard of ⑩ the **Palais Bourbon**, the home of France's Parliament, the Assemblée Nationale. Many of the important personages thus transported enjoy power lunches at ⑪ **Chez Marius** (5 rue de Bourgogne, **FF-FFFF**), where the setting is appropriately distinguished and the cuisine mainly classical. ⑫ The **Grand Hôtel de Monaco**, built in the 1770s by Alexandre-Théodore Brongniart, the neo-classical architect of the Bourse (*see page 63*), for the estranged wife of Honoré Grimaldi, Prince of Monaco, has housed at various times the embassies of Turkey, Austria and, since 1907, Poland. ⑬ The **Hôtel de Noirmoutiers**, dating from half a century earlier, witnessed in 1929 the death of the First World War generalissimo Marshal Foch; it is now the headquarters of the Institut géographique national, publisher of the superb IGN maps of France.

▲ 81

Chambre
des Députés

R. DE COURTY

R. DE L'UNIVERSITE

R. DE LILLE

R. DE SOLFÉRINO

BD ST-GERMAIN

Solférino

R. ST-DOMINIQUE

SQ.
ROUSSEAU

R. CASIMIR-PÉRIER

R. LAS CASES

R. DE BELLECHASSE

Solférino

Musee d'Orsay

▲ 71

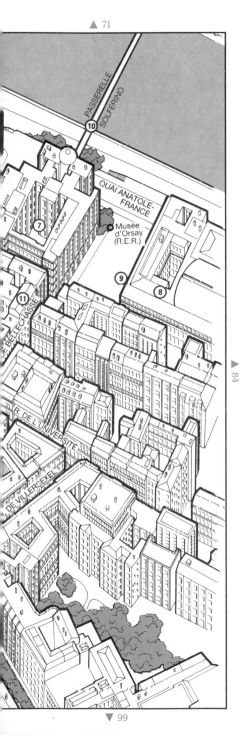

▶ 84

① Baron Hausmann's gangs of labourers started carving the **boulevard St-Germain** through the old streets on the Left Bank in 1866. A number of fine mansions survived the wholesale demolitions of the period, including ②, at No. 217 in the boulevard, what is now the **Maison de l'Amérique latine** whose restaurant (**FFF**) gives you a chance to eat out in the large tree-shaded garden. ③ The **Institut néerlandais** (entrance at 121 rue de Lille), whose collections of German as well as Dutch paintings are open to the public. ④ The **Ministère de la Défense** (Defence Ministry), one of many official buildings in the Faubourg St-Germain. Gustave Doré lived for over thirty years in ⑤ the **Hôtel de Tavennes** (5 rue St-Dominique), and died there in 1883. ⑥ The **Hôtel de Beauharnais** (78 rue de Lille), designed in 1714 by France's greatest rococo architect Gabriel Germain Boffrand, and opulently redecorated by Napoleon's step-children, Eugène de Beauharnais and Hortense, Queen of Holland, is now the residence of the German ambassador. ⑦ The **Hôtel de Salm**, where Madame de Staël held her brilliant political salon, houses the **Musée de la Légion d'honneur** (entrance at 2 rue de Bellechasse): a feast for all interested in medals and in the history of the tiny red rosette worn by holders of France's top military and civil decoration, dreamed up by Napoleon in 1802. Opposite this museum, its entrance flanked by bronze statues of a horse, an elephant and a rhinoceros, ⑧ its big brother, the **Musée d'Orsay**, once a rail station, now a stylish and very popular museum devoted to fine and applied art from the period 1848 to 1914 (Café des Hauteurs, **F**, on the top floor for snacks, full-scale restaurant, **FF**, with superbly elaborate 19thC décor on first floor). ⑨ The **RER station** beneath the museum (entrance in rue de Bellechasse) is a convenient starting-point for a trip out to Versailles (line C, trains whose identification starts with the letter V). ⑩ The **passerelle Solférino**, a footbridge leading across the Seine to the Tuileries Gardens. The rue de Bellechasse has two small restaurants well placed for a meal before or after a visit to the Musée d'Orsay: ⑪ **Le Crik** (No. 8), for light meals from about midday to 8 p.m.; and ⑫ **Aux Petits Oignons** (**FF**, No. 20), open usual mealtimes.

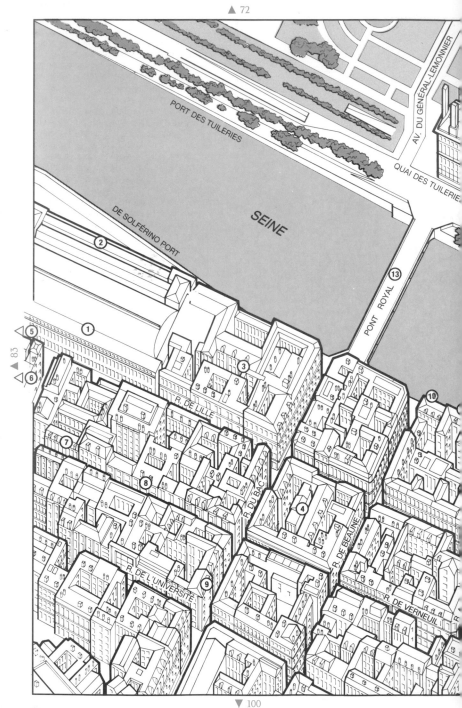

PORT DES TUILERIES

AV. DU GÉNÉRAL-LEMONNIER

QUAI DES TUILERIES

SEINE

DE SOLFÉRINO PORT

PONT ROYAL

R. DE LILLE

R. DU BAC

R. DE BEAUNE

R. DE L'UNIVERSITÉ

R. DE VERNEUIL

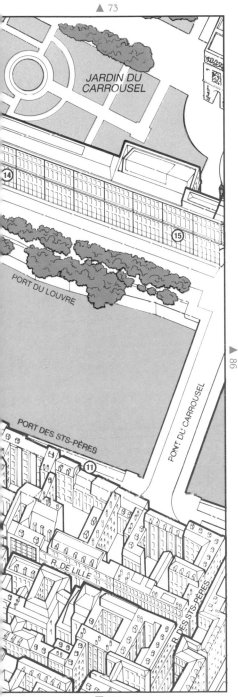

Carré Rive Gauche/ Louvre/Tuileries

① The monumental façade of the old **Gare d'Orsay** (now the Musée d'Orsay, *see page 83*), designed by Victor Laloux at the very end of the 19thC. ② The famous **Impressionist collections**, previously in the Jeu de Paume (*see page 71*), are now in the long gallery overlooking the Seine, fronted by a terrace (views up to Montmartre). ③ The **Caisse des Dépôts et des Consignations**, rebuilt after extensive fire damage during the Commune in 1871, in a mansion designed by Robert de Cotte in the early 18thC; a hundred years later George Sand and Sainte-Beuve were regular customers of the Café d'Orsay on the ground floor. ④ The many small antique shops within the squarish area formed by the rue du Bac, the rue de Lille, the rue des Saints-Pères and the rue de l'Université like to promote themselves as the **Carré Rive Gauche**. ⑤ The **Solférino at 91 rue de Lille, FF** (off map), small hotel, prettily furnished. ⑥ The **Hôtel d'Avejan** (11 rue de Poitiers), a delightful early 18thC mansion, now the home of the Centre national des Lettres, a government-funded writers' centre with ⑦ the **Café des Lettres** (entrance at 53 rue de Verneuil, **F-FF**), good for a light lunch. ⑧ For the most fashionable Vietnamese cuisine in Paris, unexpectedly accompanied by one of its finest wine lists, **Tan Dinh** (60 rue de Verneuil, **FFF**). And for superb chocolates, ⑨ **Christian Constant** (26 rue du Bac). ⑩ The **quai Voltaire** really was the home of Voltaire: he lived at No. 27, the **Hôtel de Villette**, for a year in the 1720s, then returned half a century later, at the age of eighty-three, dying there a few months later. But this is not the quai's only literary connection: Baudelaire wrote part of *Les Fleurs du Mal* at ⑪ **No. 19**, of which Wagner was a tenant three years later, and Alfred de Musset spent ten years at ⑫ **No. 25**. ⑬ The **Pont Royal** was carried away by ice masses in 1684 and rebuilt the following year by Louis XIV at his own expense, to designs by Mansart and Gabriel. It leads to ⑭ the **Pavillon de Flore**, whose foundation stone was laid by Charles IX, though the whole of ⑮ the **Galerie du Bord de l'Eau**, to which it adds a final flourish, was planned by his mother Catherine de Médicis, as a link between the Louvre and her Tuileries Palace, now vanished.

⑦

⑥
PL. DU
CARROUSEL

⑤

①

④

②

⑧

QUAI DU LOUVRE

PORT DU LOUVRE

SEINE

PORT DES STS-PÈRES

QUAI

MALAQUAIS

R. BONAPARTE

PASSERELLE DES ARTS

PL. DE
L'INSTITUT

⑩

⑫

The Louvre

▲ 75

① The elegant steel and glass **Louvre Pyramid**, Paris's most controversial eighties monument, designed by the Chinese/American architect I.M. Pei, forms the entrance to ② the main wing of the **Musée du Louvre** (Louvre Museum), probably the world's largest art collection, and to the newly excavated foundations of the medieval fortress of the Louvre, beneath ③ the **Cour Carrée**, a survivor from the royal palace planned by François I. ④ The **Pavillon de l'Horloge**, built during the reign of Louis XIII, is continued to the south by a wing designed by Pierre Lescot and decorated with carved friezes by the Renaissance sculptor Jean Goujon, best known for the lovely Fontaine des Innocents beside Les Halles (*see page 91*). ⑤ Lead replica of a marble equestrian statue of Louis XIV by Bernini, which the Sun King loathed so much that he had it converted into the figure of the Roman general Marcus Curtius flinging himself into the flames to save the Republic. ⑥ The **place du Carrousel** earned its name as a site for 17thC equestrian displays and tournaments. ⑦ At its heart, the **Arc de Triomphe du Carrousel**, built to celebrate Napoleon's victories at the Battle of Austerlitz and Jena, and now topped by a gilded bronze chariot and four by the Monégasque sculptor François Joseph Bosio, who also carved the equestrian statue of Louis XIV in the place des Victoires (*see page 77*). ⑧ The **Galerie du Bord de l'Eau**, commissioned by Catherine de Médicis to link the Louvre with her (now vanished) Tuileries Palace. ⑨ The **Passerelle des Arts**, romantically dotted with orange trees in tubs, is the latest incarnation of a footbridge known to generations of lovers as the Pont des Arts, which collapsed when a barge crashed into one of its piers in the early eighties. ⑩ From the bridge, a splendid view of the shining cupola of the **Palais de l'Institut**, built (mainly by Louis Le Vau) in the mid-17thC and housing the five academies that make up the Institut de France; best known of the five is the Académie Française, whose stern lexicographers famously ban words from their weighty *Dictionary of the French Language*. ⑪ The **bouquinistes** (second-hand bookstalls) beside the Seine are open most afternoons. ⑫ Interesting temporary exhibitions are mounted in the **école nationale supérieure des Beaux-Arts** (art academy). ⑬ (*See* ① *on page 89.*)

▶ 38

▼ 103

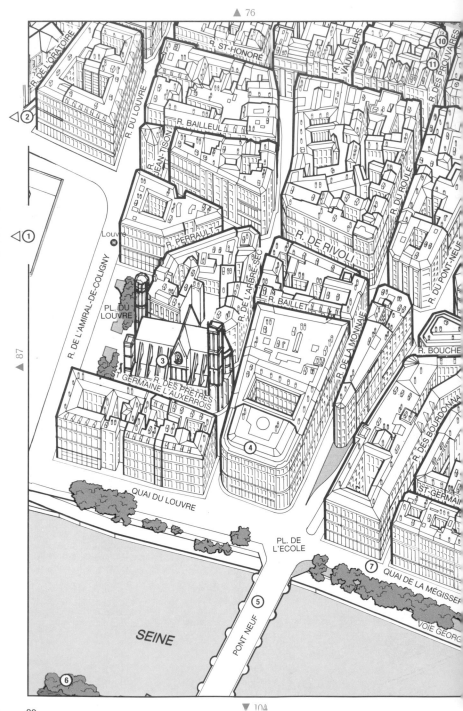

R. DE L'ORATOIRE
R. ST-HONORÉ
R. VAUVILLIERS
10
11
R. DES PROUVAIRES
2
R. DU LOUVRE
R. BAILLEUL
R. JEAN-TISON
1
R. PERRAULT
R. DE RIVOLI
R. DU ROULE
Louvre
M
R. DE L'ARBRE-SEC
R. BAILLET
R. DU PONT-NEUF
R. DE L'AMIRAL-DE-COLIGNY
PL. DU LOUVRE
R. BOUCHE
3
R. DE LA MONNAIE
R. DES PRÊTRES
GERMAINE L'AUXERROIS
R. DES BOURDONNAI
4
QUAI DU LOUVRE
ST-GERMAIN
PL. DE L'ECOLE
7
QUAI DE LA MÉGISSER
5
PONT NEUF
VOIE GEORG
SEINE
6

St-Germain-l'Auxerrois

(1) **The Louvre Colonnade**, a textbook example of French classical architecture (*see* (13) *on page 87*), designed by Claude Perrault, architect brother of the author of *Cinderella* and all the best fairy-tales. (2) **Statue of Admiral Gaspard de Coligny**, who perished during the infamous 'Massacre of St Bartholomew' (23 August 1572) instigated by Catherine de Médicis. (3) The signal for that horrific slaughter of over 3,000 Protestants was given from the belfry of **St-Germain-de-l'Auxerrois**, long the parish church of the kings of France. (4) **La Samaritaine**, a sprawling department store with a famous roof terrace (sweeping views over the Seine and the Left Bank), founded by Ernest Cognacq, who with his wife Louise Jay amassed the 18thC art collection that forms the nucleus of the Musée Cognacq-Jay (*see page 95*). (5) The store's name comes from a sculpture of Christ by the well with the Woman of Samaria that used to adorn a huge pump building beside the **Pont Neuf**, started in 1578 and once lined with tall houses. (6) One of the landing stages for the Seine sightseeing boats (*see page 19*) is in the leafy **square du Vert-Galant**, a popular spot for strolling lovers. (7) The **Quai de la Mégisserie** is Paris's Pets' Corner – a long string of little shops selling live birds, rabbits and goldfish. (8) **Le Châtelet Gourmand** (**FF**, 13 rue des Lavandières-Ste-Opportune), a cheerful little bistrot, often crowded with patrons of (9) the **Théâtre du Châtelet**, a grand 19thC playhouse known for its musicals. (10) **Le Louchébem** (**FF**, 10 rue des Prouvaires), specializes in meat – hence its name, meaning 'butcher' in the curious Paris argot used in and around the old central food market and known to philologists as 'butchers' slang'. (11) In the same street (No. 5) **La Tour de Monthléry** (**FFF**), another crowded bistrot with something of the atmosphere of the old Halles.

▼ 106

Les Halles/Beaubourg/Châtelet

① The **Forum des Halles**, a sleek glass-and-concrete shopping and entertainment centre, has replaced the eastern end of the centuries-old food market. ② The **Fontaine des Innocents**, Renaissance fountain adorned with superb watery nymphs by Jean Goujon. The square surrounding it is packed day and night with a lively crowd, many of them busy seeing and being seen at a strategic table in ③ the **Café Costes**, decked out in fifties style by oh so-chic designer Philippe Starck. ④ **Le Bistro d'Eustache** (37 rue Berger, off map, **FF**), one of dozens of lively restaurants in and around Les Halles. ⑤ Henri IV was assassinated on 14 May 1610 outside **11 rue de la Ferronerie** by a schoolteacher called Ravaillac. ⑥ The **rue St-Denis**, a red-light district for centuries, now lined with 'in' restaurants like ⑦ **Joe Allen** (30 rue Pierre-Lescot, **FF**), popular with homesick American expats and trend-conscious French. Also definitely 'in', ⑧ **Pacific Palisades** (51 rue Quincampoix, **FF**). ⑨ **Constantin Brâncuşi's studio** can be visited on the northern edge of ⑩ the **Piazza**, a sloping area thronged with street entertainers enlivening the wait of queues to get into ⑪ the **Centre national d'Art et de Culture Georges-Pompidou**, better known as the Centre Beaubourg, housing the **Musée national d'Art Moderne** (Modern Art Museum). Once arousing fierce passions with its determinedly 'inside-out' design and its shrieking colours, it now seems part of the landscape. ⑫ The **Quartier de l'Horloge** has a timepiece-cum-sculpture whose automated figures play out a symbolic battle on the stroke of each new hour. ⑬ **L'Ambassade d'Auvergne** (off map at 22 rue du Grenier-Saint-Lazare, **FF**), a reliable place to enjoy hearty cuisine from the Massif Central. ⑭ The early 18thC **Fontaine Maubuée**, decorated with aquatic plants spilling out of a vase and the proud sailing ship that features on Paris's coat of arms. ⑮ Brilliantly coloured animated sculptures by Jean Tinguely and Niki de Saint-Phalle form the **Fontaine Stravinsky**, in a square overlooked by ⑯ **St-Merri**, built in richly decorated Late Gothic style, but dating from the early 17thC. ⑰ **Le Chant des voyelles**, a complicated piece by the Cubist sculptor Jacques Lipchitz. ⑱ **La Cloche à Fromages** (25 rue de La Reynie, **F-FF**), specializing, as the name suggests, in cheese dishes. ⑲ The **Tour Saint-Jacques**, a good example of 'Flamboyant' Gothic.

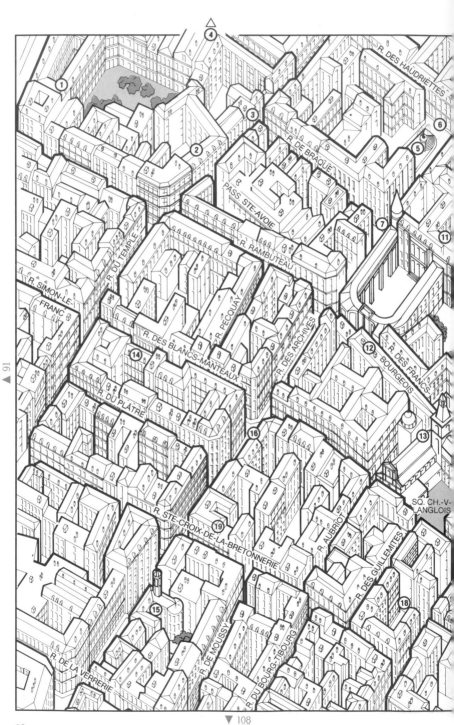

The Archives Nationales

① In the tiny Impasse Berthaud, perhaps the most delightful of Paris's specialist museums, the **Musée des Instruments de Musique mécanique**, devoted to barrel organs, musical boxes and the like, all in perfect working order. ② After extensive restoration, the **Hôtel de St-Aignan**, built in 1640 for the Comte d'Avaux, French ambassador to the Netherlands, Venice, England and Sweden, will house the **Musée d'Art juif** (Jewish Art Museum), previously in Montmartre. ③ The **Hôtel de Montmor** is a couple of decades earlier; Descartes and Molière frequented a literary academy there. ④ At 3 rue Volta (off map), the **oldest house in Paris**, dating from 1292. ⑤ The 18thC **Fontaine des Haudriettes**, adorned with a naiad by Mignot. ⑥ The lively **Connétable** (55 rue des Archives, **FF**) offers good (mainly fish) cuisine and traditional French songs in the cellars of a house that once belonged to the Cardinal de Retz, who instigated the Fronde rebellion in 1648. ⑦ But the restaurant takes its name from a famous knight, the Connétable Olivier de Clisson, who fought alongside the great Du Guesclin; the **turreted Gothic doorway of his manorhouse** has survived at 58 rue des Archives. ⑧ The **Hôtel Guénégaud**, designed by François Mansart, now the **Musée de la Chasse et de la Nature** (Hunting and Natural History Museum), whose formal garden can be seen from ⑨ the **rue des Quatre-Fils**, named after a tavern sign depicting the heroes of a medieval romance, *Les Quatre Fils Aymon*. At Nos 11-13 in the same street, ⑩ the striking modern premises of **CARAN**, the acronym for the computerized research centre (open to the public) attached to ⑪ the **Archives Nationales** (National Document Centre), in the imposing 18thC **Palais Rohan-Soubise**. Also in the palace, the **Musée de l'Histoire de France** (French History Museum), and the rococo rooms lived in by the Prince and Princesse de Soubise. ⑫ **Le Dômarais** (53 rue des Francs-Bourgeois, **FF**), fashionably light cuisine in the unexpected setting of a pawnbroker's showroom. ⑬ **Nôtre-Dame-des-Blancs-Manteaux** has a magnificent carved and inlaid 18thC pulpit. ⑭ **La Petite Chaumière** (41 rue des Blancs-Manteaux, **FF**), cosy restaurant popular with locals. ⑮ The **Cloître des Billettes**, medieval cloisters. ⑯ The medieval financier-diplomat Jacques Coeur lived at **42 rue des Archives**. ⑰ On the **Hôtel Hérouet**, dating from 1528, a (somewhat over-restored) medieval turret has survived. ⑱ Beaumarchais wrote *The Marriage of Figaro* in the **Hôtel des Ambassadeurs de Hollande**. ⑲ **Bretonnerie** (**FF**), hotel in a 17thC house. ⑳ See ② , page 95.

▲ 94

Musée Picasso

(1) **La Taverne des Templiers** (106 rue Vieille-du-Temple, **FF**), overdone medieval décor but smiling service and tasty cuisine from the Charente region. (2) The **Hôtel de Rohan**, built for the Prince-Bishops of Strasbourg by the same architect as the Palais Soubise (*see page 93*), with which it shares a garden, is famous for the superb carving of *The Horses of the Sun* by Robert Le Lorrain over the stable doors. (3) The **Hôtel Aubert de Fontenay** or **Hôtel Salé** makes an unexpectedly effective setting for the **Musée Picasso** (small restaurant). (4) Balzac went to school in the same street, at **7 rue de Thorigny**. (5) The **Musée de la Serrure** (Museum of Locks and Locksmiths), in the **Hôtel Libéral Bruant**, built for the architect who designed Les Invalides (*see page 97*). (6) The **Musée Cognacq-Jay**, previously in the boulevard des Capucines, has moved to the **Hôtel Donon**; 18thC furniture and paintings. (7) The **square Georges-Caïn**, with a graceful late 17thC bronze *Flora* by Laurent Magnier, commemorates a keeper of the Musée Carnavalet (*see page 111*). The museum celebrated the bicentenary of the French Revolution in style by opening an extension to house its revolutionary collections in (8) the **Hôtel-Le-Peletier-de-St-Fargeau**, the home of an aristocratic family, one of whose members was assassinated because he had voted for the death of Louis XVI. (9) The **Swedish Cultural Centre** (frequent art exhibitions), in the late 16thC **Hôtel de Marle**, lived in at one time by Marie-Antoinette's favourite, Madame de Polignac, whom she appointed governess to her children. Opposite (10) the well-kept little garden in the **square Louis-Achille**, the courtyard of (11) the **Hôtel de Vigny**, in which some early 17thC painted beams have survived, along with a superb ceiling painted with scenes depicting the seasons and the four elements. In the rue de Turenne: (12) the **Hôtel du Grand-Veneur** or **Hôtel d'Ecquevilly**, with a proud boar's head over the garden façade and a beautiful staircase, oddly used to display bathroom and other furnishings (No. 60); (13) the **Fontaine de Joyeuse** (No. 41), a 19thC tribute to the river Ourcq. (14) At **No. 54**, an elegant façade on what is now a school. (15) A major work by Delacroix – a *Deposition* painted straight on to a chapel wall – is the most interesting feature of the 19thC **St-Denis-du-St-Sacrament**, modelled on a Roman basilica.

SQ. D'AJACCIO

Varenne

R. DE VARENNE

BD DES INVALIDES

AV. DE TOURVILLE

PL. VAUBAN

AV. DE VILLARS

Les Invalides

96 ▶

① The vast façade of the **Hôtel des Invalides**, commissioned from Libéral Bruant by Louis XIV to house wounded or elderly ex-soldiers, is overshadowed by the splendidly regilded cupola of ② the **Eglise du Dôme**, built by Jules Hardouin-Mansart, now housing **Napoleon's Tomb** – his remains were ceremoniously brought back from St Helena in 1840. The complex of buildings forming Les Invalides also includes ③ a second church, **St-Louis-des-Invalides**, bedecked with the tattered flags seized during Napoleon's many campaigns. *Son-et-lumière* performances conjuring up the return of his remains (about Easter to Oct) are staged in ④ the **Cour d'honneur**, round which classical buildings, adorned with an equestrian statue of the Sun King above the central doorway, are the home of ⑤ the **Musée de l'Armée** (Military Museum). This large and important museum has various annexes: the **Musée des Plans-Reliefs** (Relief Maps Museum), displaying scale models of fortified towns throughout France, some of them dating back to the 17thC; the **Musée des Deux Guerres mondiales** (World Wars Museum); and ⑥ the **Musée de l'Ordre de la Libération** (entrance at 51bis boulevard de Latour-Maubourg, off map), devoted to the élite among General de Gaulle's 'Companions' (not necessarily in arms) decorated with the medal he instituted in the dark days of 1940. A fine view of the dome can be enjoyed from ⑦ the **Jardin de l'Intendant** beside the church (just off map), featuring a statue of Hardouin-Mansart by Ernest Dubois, or from ⑧ the **place Vauban**, whose own statues, of the First World War heroes Marshal Galliéni and Marshal Fayolle, are far less pleasing. For sculpture of the highest order, cross ⑨ the **boulevard des Invalides** to ⑩ the **Hôtel Biron**, a fine 18thC mansion whose gardens and beautiful rooms display the work of Auguste Rodin (entrance to the **Musée Rodin** is at 77 rue de Varenne). ⑪ **L'Arpège** (**FF-FFFF**, 84 rue de Varenne) has pulled off the difficult feat of following Alain Senderens's *Archestrate* when it moved to the Madeleine (*see pages 56-57*): deliciously light cuisine, remarkable-value lunch *menu*. ⑫ **Varenne** (**FF**, 44 rue de Bourgogne), charming little hotel with a tiny patio-courtyard for summer breakfasts.

R. DE GRENELLE

R. BELLECHASSE

① ② R. DE VARENNE

R. VANEAU

▲ 97

⑤
▽

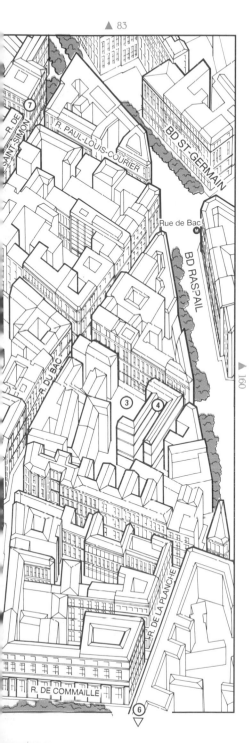

Faubourg St-Germain

① The early 18thC **Hôtel Matignon** (57 rue de Varenne), the official residence of the prime minister, with Paris's largest private garden, was once the home of the prelate-turned-diplomat/statesman Talleyrand, who was himself briefly prime minister during the second restoration of the monarchy - and allegedly remarked that 'war is much too serious a matter to be left to the military'. ② At No. 47 in the same street, the **Italian Embassy**, in the **Hôtel de Boisgelin**: Monsignor Boisgelin, the former archbishop of Aix, built on to the early 18thC ground floor half a century later. ③ The highly decorative **Fontaine des Quatre-Saisons** or **Fontaine Bouchardon** (57 rue de Grenelle) features the City of Paris flanked by river deities representing the Seine and the Marne, while cupids looking like mischievous children till the fields and reap the corn following the rhythm of the seasons. It was commissioned from the sculptor Edme Bouchardon in the 1730s, when the inhabitants of the increasingly fashionable Faubourg-St-Germain were starting to protest at constant water shortages. Alfred de Musset wrote several of his sparkling plays in a house in the courtyard of ④ the **Hôtel Bouchardon** (No. 59), which is slowly being converted into a museum of modern art, the **Musée Dina Vierny** (the lady in question was one of Aristide Maillol's models). ⑤ The **Hôtel de la Vallière** (136 rue du Bac, off map) has belonged since 1813 to the Sisters of Charity, the order founded by St Vincent de Paul, whose convent is in the same *îlot* or block of buildings. The Virgin Mary allegedly appeared at least five times in its chapel to a former dairy-maid, Catherine Labouré: during one of these visions she showed the girl a medal and told her to have it copied (twenty million medals were subsequently sold). ⑥ **La Cigale** (11 bis rue Chomel, off map, **FF**), a good place for savouring *cuisine bourgeoise* in a bistrot atmosphere. For a chic ambiance presided over (occasionally) by a glamorous television presenter and her chef husband, ⑦ **La Ferme St-Simon** (6 rue St-Simon, **FF-FFFF**).

R. MONTALEMBERT

R. SÉBASTIEN-BOTTIN

③ ④

⑤

⑧

⑥

R. DE GRIBEAUVAL

⑦

R. DU PRÉ-AUX-CLERCS

R. ST-TOMAS-D'AQUIN

PL. ST-THOMAS-D'AQUIN

⑯

⑰

R. DE LUYNES

BD ST-GERMAIN

②

R. ST-GUILLAUME

⑬

⑪

⑫

R. DE GRENELLE

R. DES SAINTS-PÈRES

①

BD RASPAIL

R. DE LA CHAISE

SQ. CHAISE
RÉCAMIER

Rue du Bac/Université

▲ 85

① The sign hanging up outside **La Petite Chaise** (36 rue de Grenelle, **FF**), said to be Paris's oldest restaurant, dates from 1681. ② Guillaume Apollinaire lived at **202 boulevard St-Germain**, dying there, at only thirty-eight, in 1918, the year in which his *Calligrammes* appeared. He had never recovered from a head wound received at the front two years earlier, but was essentially a victim of that year's deadly Spanish flu epidemic. Writers and their publishers traditionally congregate in the bars of two well-known and well-run hotels side by side in the rue Montalembert: ③ the **Montalembert** (No. 3, **FF-FFF**), with spacious thirties rooms, and ④ the **Pont-Royal** (No. 7, **FFF**), the name of whose restaurant, *Les Antiquaires*, reflects the preponderance of antique shops in the streets leading to the Seine. But this is essentially a book-publishing stronghold, with ⑤ **Editions Gallimard** (in the little rue Sébastien-Bottin) still France's most prestigious house, in spite of some very public family feuding in recent years. ⑥ Romain Gary, diplomat, novelist and husband of Jean Seberg, who pulled off the extraordinary feat of winning the Prix Goncourt, France's top book prize, twice (once under a pseudonym) lived for many years in the **rue du Bac**, where he committed suicide on 2 December 1980. ⑦ **St-Thomas-d'Aquin**, originally called St-Dominique, designed in the 1680s by the classical architect Pierre Bullet in the Jesuit style, in the shape of a Greek cross, for the Dominicans whose monastery buildings spread over the surrounding streets. The high-flying alumni of ⑧ the **Ecole nationale d'Administration** or ENA (13 rue de l'Université) are known as *énarques*. ⑨ Another élite *grande école*, the **Ecole nationale des Ponts et Chaussées**. Its entrance is at No. 28 in ⑩ the **rue des Saints-Pères**, which has two long-popular hotels: ⑪ the **Pas-de-Calais** (No. 59, **FF**), and ⑫ the **Saints-Pères** (**No. 65, FF-FFF**), both with inner courtyard-gardens for lazy summer breakfasts. ⑬ Opposite at No. 54, the **Musée-Bibliothèque du Protestantisme français** offers an interesting glimpse into the persecution of the Protestants, whose mobile pulpits (designed to be speedily folded up and whisked out of sight) are on display. ⑭ The **rue Bernard-Palissy** has kept most of its 17thC houses and ⑮ at No. 7, **Editions de Minuit**, publishers of Samuel Beckett and the exponents of the *nouveau roman*. ⑯ Militaria bibliophiles converge on **Librairie Pierre Petitot** (254 boulevard St-Germain), while umbrella freaks have been making their way to ⑰ **Madeleine Gély**, at No. 218, since 1834.

▶ 102

▼ 115

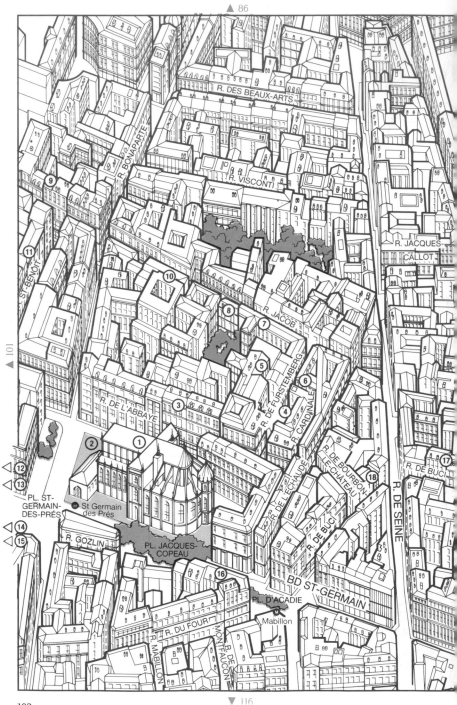

R. DES BEAUX-ARTS

R. BONAPARTE

⑨

R. VISCONTI

R. JACQUES-CALLOT

⑪

R. ST-BENOÎT

⑩

⑧

R. JACOB

⑦

⑤

R. DE FURSTEMBERG

⑥

③

R. DE L'ABBAYE

④

R. CARDINALE

② ①

⑰

R. DE BUCI

⑫

⑬

R. DE L'ÉCHAUDÉ

R. DE BOURBON-LE-CHÂTEAU

⑱

R. DE SEINE

PL. ST-GERMAIN-DES-PRÉS

Ⓜ St Germain des Prés

R. DE BUCI

⑭

⑮

R. GOZLIN

PL. JACQUES-COPEAU

BD ST-GERMAIN

⑯

PL. D'ACADIE

Ⓜ Mabillon

R. DU FOUR

R. DE MONTFAUCON

R. MABILLON

St-Germain-des-Prés

① The mainly Romanesque **church of St-Germain-des-Prés**, on the foundations of a monastery church consecrated by St Germanus, Bishop of Paris, in 1558. ② Picasso's **Homage to Apollinaire**, the centrepiece of a tiny garden adorned with architectural fragments from the church's original Lady Chapel, built by the master mason of Notre Dame, Pierre de Montereau or Montreuil (d. 1267). ③ **Réunion des Mussées Nationaux boutique**, selling museum catalogues and reproductions of exhibits (10 rue de l'Abbaye). ④ **Place Fürstemberg**, the perfect small-scale Parisian square, complete with globe lamps and catalpa trees, houses ⑤ the intimate **Musée Delacroix**, where the painter lived, worked and died (in 1863). ⑥ **Manuel Canovas** (Nos 5 and 7) for expensive and beautiful furnishing fabrics. ⑦ **Librairie Maritime d'Outre-Mer** (17 rue Jacob), a bookshop with an international nautical flavour. ⑧ **Hôtel des Marronniers (FF**, No. 21) and ⑨ **Hôtel d'Angleterre (FFF**, No. 44), with, respectively, a peaceful leafy garden and an inner patio-courtyard, are just two of St-Germain's many *hôtels de charme*. ⑩ **La Villa (FFF**, No. 27), is rather different — sleek and hi-tech. ⑪ In a street made up almost entirely of restaurants, **Le Petit St-Benoît (F**, 4 rue St-Benoît), famous for its *plats du jour* and dating back to the 1860s. ⑫ **Aux Deux Magots** (170 boulevard St-Germain), archetypal St-Germain café, attracting a mixture of tourists and intellectuals, who buy their books right up to midnight next door at ⑬ **Librairie La Hune**. ⑭ The **Café Flore** (No. 172, off map), like the Deux Magots, is still haunted by the ghosts of Sartre and Simone de Beauvoir. ⑮ **Brasserie Lipp (FFF**, No. 151, off map), a Paris institution whose hallowed ground floor is politely but firmly restricted to celebrities (the upper floor is more accessible). ⑯ **La Gaminerie** (No. 137), busy fashion boutique with a sculpted bronze entrance. ⑰ *Le tout St-Germain* do their food shopping in the **rue de Buci street market**. ⑱ **CCA, La Charcuterie alsacienne** (10 rue de Buci), the Paris branch of Alsace's most upmarket delicatessen, founded in Mulhouse in 1876. ⑲ **Café Procope (F-FFF**, 13 rue de l'Ancienne-Comédie), opened in 1686 as a coffee house, now a chic and busy restaurant with décor on the theme of the French Revolution. Its rear door leads into ⑳ the **cour du Commerce St-André**, a picturesque cobbled alleyway where Marat had his newspaper *L'Ami du Peuple* printed (at No. 8). ㉑ The late 18thC **Hôtel des Monnaies** (Mint), with a stylish new (1988) coins and medals museum (11 quai de Conti).

▲ 104

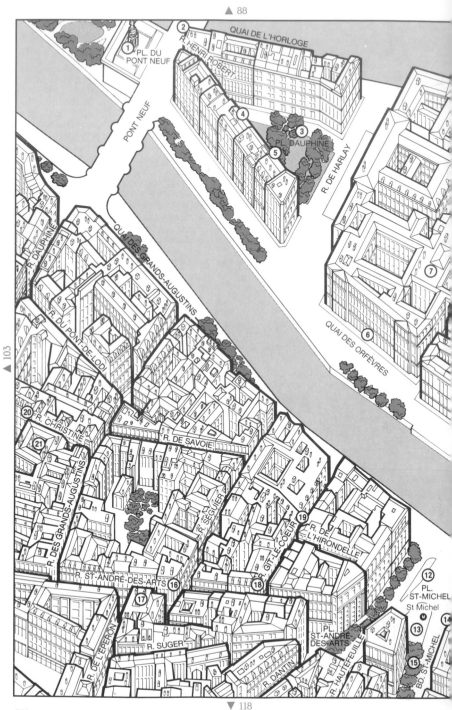

PL. DU PONT NEUF

QUAI DE L'HORLOGE

R. HENRI ROBERT

PL. DAUPHINE

R. DE HARLAY

PONT NEUF

QUAI DES GRANDS-AUGUSTINS

QUAI DES ORFÈVRES

R. DAUPHINE

R. DU PONT-DE-LODI

R. CHRISTINE

R. DE SAVOIE

R. DES GRANDS-AUGUSTINS

R. SÉGUIER

GÎT-LE-CŒUR

R. DE L'HIRONDELLE

R. ST-ANDRÉ-DES-ARTS

PL. ST-MICHEL

St Michel

R. DE L'ÉPERON

R. SUGER

R. DANTIN

PL. ST-ANDRÉ-DES-ARTS

R. HAUTEFEUILLE

BD. ST-MICHEL

Ile de la Cité/St-Michel

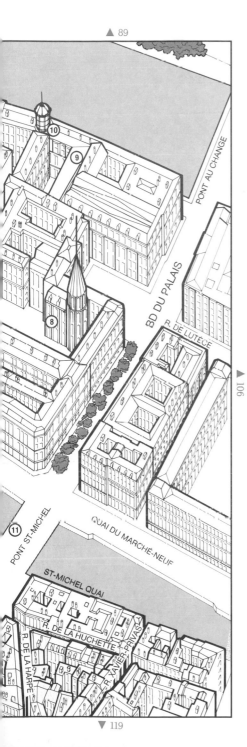

▲ 89

▶ 106

▼ 119

① An **equestrian statue of Henri IV** in the place du Pont-Neuf gazes thoughtfully towards ② the **Taverne Henri IV** (No. 13), an atmospheric wine bar. ③ The peaceful 17thC **place Dauphine**, named after the then *dauphin*, the infant Louis XIII, with a couple of tea rooms, ④ **Le Caveau du Palais** (Nos 17-19, **FFF**), a wine bar plus restaurant frequented by lawyers, and ⑤ **Paul** (No. 15, **FF**), often described as the archetypal Paris bistrot, which has a riverside entrance on ⑥ the **quai des Orfèvres**, the name familiarly used for the *Police judiciaire*, France's crime investigation department. Its headquarters are further east along the *quai*, in the huge complex dominated by ⑦ the **Palais de Justice** (law courts). Also in the complex of buildings, once the royal palace, ⑧ the superb Gothic **Sainte Chapelle**, built by Pierre de Montereau (also known as de Montreuil) for Louis IX, to house the sacred relics he had bought from the Emperor of Constantinople. Binoculars are an asset when you try to decipher the hundreds of biblical scenes depicted in the glorious stained glass in the Chapelle Haute (upper chapel). On the river side, the towers of ⑨ the medieval **Conciergerie** stand guard over what was once an infamous prison, its most celebrated inmate Queen Marie-Antoinette, before the tumbril took her to the guillotine. ⑩ The earliest of the towers is the **Tour Bonbec**, built in about 1250, and later used as a torture chamber. Beyond ⑪ the **Pont St-Michel**, which, like the Pont Neuf (*see page 89*), was once lined with houses, ⑫ the ever-crowded **place St-Michel**. At its heart, ⑬ the **Fontaine St-Michel**, an elaborate concoction decorated with pink marble pillars featuring the archangel Michael flinging the devil into the waters of the fountain, commissioned by Baron Haussmann from the architect Gabriel Davioud and a magnet for youthful revellers. ⑭ **Gibert Jeune**, a large academic bookshop, is a magnet of a different sort, at the river end of ⑮ the busy **boulevard St-Michel**, which lost its paving stones after they had been used as missiles during the 1968 'May Events'. Racine lived at No. 41 in ⑯ the lively **rue St-André-des-Arts**, now ⑰ the well-known bistrot **Allard** (**FFFF**). The mistress of François I, the Duchesse d'Etampes lived in a richly furnished mansion in ⑱ the **rue Gît-le-Coeur**, frequented by the fifties Beat Generation staying in the picturesque ⑲ **Hôtel du Vieux-Paris** (**F**). Picasso painted *Guernica* in the rue des Grands-Augustins, opposite ⑳ the **rue Christine**, where 16thC cloisters have been converted into ㉑ the peaceful and elegant **Relais Christine** hotel (No. 3, **FFF**).

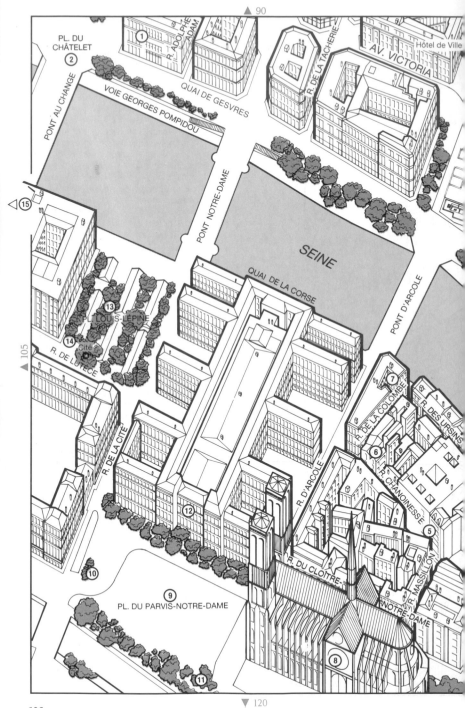

PL. DU CHÂTELET
②
①
R. ADOLPHE ADAM.
QUAI DE GESVRES
PONT AU CHANGE
VOIE GEORGES POMPIDOU
R. DE LA TACHERIE
AV. VICTORIA
Hôtel de Ville
PONT NOTRE-DAME
⑮
SEINE
QUAI DE LA CORSE
⑬
PL. LOUIS-LÉPINE
PONT D'ARCOLE
⑭
Cité
R. DE LUTECE
105
R. DE LA CITÉ
⑦
R. DE LA COLOMBE
R. DES URSINS
⑥
R. CHANOINESSE
⑫
R. D'ARCOLE
⑤
R. MASSILLON
⑩
R. DU CLOÎTRE
NOTRE-DAME
⑨
PL. DU PARVIS-NOTRE-DAME
⑧
⑪
90
120

Hôtel de Villes

Hôtel de Villes

③

④

QUAI DE L'HÔTEL-DE-VILLE

VOIE GEORGES-POMPI

R. DE LOBAU

R. DES CHANTRES

QUAI AUX FLEURS

PONT ST-LOUIS

▶ 108

Hôtel de Ville/Notre Dame

① The **Théâtre de la Ville**, one of two vast 19thC playhouses in ② the **place du Châtelet**, once resounded to the thrilling voice of its director, the great Sarah Bernhardt. The figures perched high up on ③ the **Hôtel de Ville** (Town Hall) are, like the rest of the façade, copies of the Renaissance structure burnt to the ground during the Paris Commune. But the first seat of the city council on this site was 14thC, presided over by ④ Etienne Marcel, the 'Provost of the Merchants', whose **equestrian statue**, brandishing a sword, overlooks the river. ⑤ The romantic story of Abélard and Héloïse was played out in the **rue Chanoinesse**, one of only a handful of narrow medieval streets that survived Baron Haussmann's wholesale demolitions on the Ile de la Cité. ⑥ At No. 24, **La Lieutenance** (**FFFF**), overpriced but atmospheric, in an ivy-covered house once lived in by a medieval canon of Notre Dame. Also well on the tourist beat, ⑦ **La Colombe** (4 rue de la Colombe, **FF**), oozing with medieval charm and peopled with white doves. ⑧ The majestic Gothic **cathedral of Notre Dame** was once only one of dozens of churches on the island. By banishing cars and coaches from ⑨ the **place du Parvis Notre Dame**, the huge square in front of the cathedral, the planners have enabled you to admire in peace the intricately carved west front, with its three great portals, much of whose sculpture dates from the sweeping 19thC restoration embarked on by Viollet-le-Duc, with the urgent encouragement of Victor Hugo and Ingres. ⑩ The **Crypte archéologique**, a museum-with-a-difference. Its exhibits the archaeological remains and countless objects that came to light during excavations beneath the square. ⑪ Bronze **statue of Charlemagne**, cast for one of the 19thC's many 'World's Exhibitions', his horse led by those soldierly heroes of romance, Roland and Oliver. This site was once filled with a hospice dating back to the 7thC, whose name has been preserved in ⑫ the 19thC **Hôtel Dieu**, a large hospital on the other side of the square. On the edge of ⑬ the **place Louis-Lépine**, famous for its flower market (Mon-Sat) and its Sunday caged bird market ⑭ is a rare survivor: one of the arching art nouveau **Métro entrances** designed by Hector Guimard. ⑮ The **Tour de l'Horloge** on the south-eastern corner of the Conciergerie (off map, *see page 105*) boasts the earliest public clock in Paris, over six centuries old and still in working order.

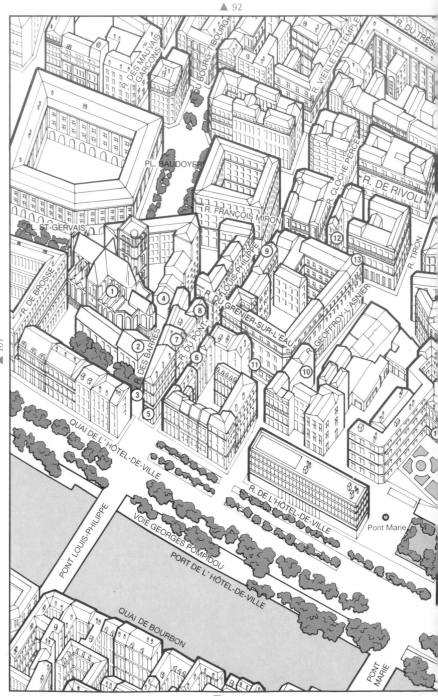

R. DU TRÉSO

R. DES MAUVAIS GARÇONS

DU BOURG-TIBOURG

R. VIEILLE DU TEMPLE

PL. BAUDOYER

R. DE RIVOLI

R. CLOCHE PERCE

R. FRANÇOIS MIRON

PL. ST-GERVAIS

R. DE BROSSE

R. LOUIS-PHILIPPE

R. TIRON

⑫

⑨

⑬

①

④

⑧

R. DU GRENIER-SUR-L'EAU

R. GEOFFROY-L'ASNIER

⑦

②

R. DES BARRES

R. DU PONT

⑥

⑪

⑩

③

⑤

QUAI DE L'HÔTEL-DE-VILLE

R. DE L'HÔTEL-DE-VILLE

Ⓜ Pont Marie

PONT LOUIS-PHILIPPE

VOIE GEORGES POMPIDOU

PORT DE L'HÔTEL-DE-VILLE

QUAI DE BOURBON

PONT MARIE

St-Gervais-St-Protais/ the southern Marais

① The classical tiered façade of **the church of St-Gervais-St-Protais** is attributed to Salomon de Brosse, the architect of the Luxembourg Palace (*see page 127*). Its fine organ, played by François Couperin and his family for generations, is regularly used for concerts. ② The entrance to the church's old **charnel house** can be seen at No. 15 in ③ the picturesque **rue des Barres**, one of whose medieval buildings houses surely the most attractive youth hostel in France, ④ the **Accueil des Jeunes en France** in the Hôtel Maubuisson (No. 12). ⑤ **Chez Julien** (1 rue du Pont-Louis-Philippe, **FF**), an old baker's converted into a restaurant. Another example of the recent transformation of many of the Marais's shops can be seen round the corner at ⑥ **No. 6**, where a *charcuterie-traiteur* has become a design boutique. Also in the rue du Pont-Louis-Philippe, ⑦ **Papier Plus** (No. 9) for stylish stationery and ⑧ **Le Grenier sur l'Eau** (No. 14, **FF**), elegant and intimate, mostly traditional cuisine. ⑨ **Marie Touchet's house** (No. 22bis), with a tiny Renaissance courtyard, was bought by the beautiful, cultured and unusually discreet mistress of Charles IX, who succumbed to melancholia, ordered the Massacre of St Bartholomew (*see page 89*) and died at only 24. ⑩ The early 17th **Hôtel Châlons Luxembourg** (26 rue Geoffroy-l'Asnier) has a superb doorway surmounted by a huge lion's head. ⑪ **Memorial to the Unknown Jewish Martyr**, with a small reading room and exhibits connected with the sufferings of the local Jewish community during the Second World War. ⑫ The **rue François-Miron** has a pair of crooked medieval houses (Nos 11 and 13) and several elegant mansions. ⑬ The **Maison d'Ourscamp** (Nos 44-6), with a fine Gothic cellar, houses an association dedicated to saving Paris's historic buildings (books and street plans for sale). ⑭ The **Hôtel de Beauvais** (No. 68), built for Anne of Austria's lady-in-waiting and confidante Catherine Bellier, who had earned the queen's gratitude (and largesse) by proving beyond all doubt that the youthful Louis XIV did not share his father's frequent impotence. ⑮ The **Hôtel d'Aumont** (7 rue de Jouy), a large 17thC mansion decorated by Simon Vouet and Charles Le Brun, with a noble façade by François Mansart. On the corner of the rue de Jouy and the rue de Fourcy ⑯ an old **carving of a knifegrinder** at work, originally in the rue des Nonnains-d'Hyères, which leads to ⑰ the turreted **Hôtel de Sens**, a mixture of late medieval and Renaissance architecture (entrance at 1 rue du Figuier), now housing an art library.

▲ 94

R. PAVÉE

R. DES FRANCS-BOURGEOIS

㉑

㉒

R. DES ROSIERS

R. MALHER

R. DE SÉVIGNÉ

⑱

R. DU ROI-
DE-SICILE

PL. DU MARCHÉ-
STE-CATHERINE

R. D'ORMESSON

R. NECKER

⑲

⑳

R. DE TURENNE

⑮

▲ 109

R. CARON

⑦

②

⑥

R. CHARLEMAGNE

R. ST-ANTOINE

R. DE BIRAG

◁ ①

R. DE L'HÔTEL
ST PAUL

R. NEUVE-ST-PIERRE

③

④

⑤

R. CHARLES-V

R. BEAUTREILLIS

R. DU PETIT-MUSC

110

▼ 124   La Maraicher #6

Place des Vosges

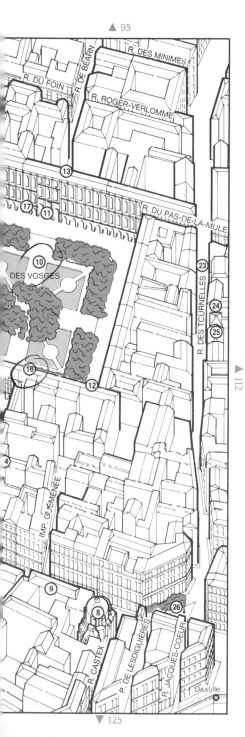

① A long stretch of the **medieval city wall** built by Philippe Auguste (off map) has oddly survived in the playground used by pupils of ② the **Lycée Charlemagne**, briefly attended by Balzac. ③ The interlocking courtyards forming the **Village Saint-Paul** are full of antique and craft shops. In the rue Charles-V, ④ **L'Excuse** (No. 14, **FF**), a discreet restaurant and ⑤ the **Hôtel d'Aubray** (No. 12), the home of that most cold-blooded of poisoners the Marquise de Brinvilliers. ⑥ The elegant **Hôtel de Sully**, built by Jean Androuet de Cerceau, now houses the Caisse nationale des Monuments historiques (Historic Buildings Commission, good bookshop). ⑦ **St-Paul-St-Louis**, built for the Jesuits in the early 17thC, has one of Delacroix's rare religious paintings, a *Christ in the Garden*. Madame de Sévigné worshipped there, but was buried in ⑧ **Ste-Marie-de-la-Visitation**, an early example of François Mansart's work, clearly influenced by Italian Baroque. ⑨ The **Hôtel de Mayenne**, again by Du Cerceau, built in brick and stone with a tall slate roof, as are the 39 uniform houses in ⑩ the lovely **place des Vosges**. Originally the place Royale, it was built by Henri IV and for over a century was the heart of an ultra-fashionable district filled with magnificent mansions. No monarch ever lived in ⑪ the **Pavillon de la Reine**. But Madame de Sévigné was born at No. 1bis and Richelieu owned No. 21. Also at No. 6 is ⑫ **Victor Hugo's House**, a museum devoted to the great man, who lived there for sixteen years from 1832, the year he wrote *Le Roi s'amuse*, on which the libretto for *Rigoletto* is based. The square is bounded north and south by pleasant hotels, ⑬ the elegant **Pavillon de la Reine (FFF)** and ⑭ the **place des Vosges** (12 rue de Birague, **FF**), and surrounded by restaurants: ⑮ **L'Ambroisie** (No. 9, **FFFF**), a revered 'temple of gastronomy'; ⑯ **Coconnas** (No. 2bis, **FF-FFF**) and ⑰ **La Guirlande de Julie** (No. 25, **FF-FFF**), both with sought-after terraces; and ⑱ the ever-popular **Ma Bourgogne** (No. 19, **FF**), for *saucisson de Beaujolais*, tripe and *foie gras*. Also surrounded by restaurants is ⑲ the tiny **place du Marché-St-Catherine**. ⑳ **Pitchi Poï (F)**, a place to try *carpe à la Juive* and other Jewish specialities, is one of the liveliest. ㉑ The **Musée Carnavalet**, with a Renaissance façade by Pierre Lescot decorated with sculptures by Jean Goujon. ㉒ The **Hôtel Lamoignon**, whose literary *salons* Racine and Boileau liked to frequent, houses a history library. ㉗, ㉔, ㉕ *See* ①, ② and ③, *page 131*. ㉖ *See* ⑤, *page 131*.

Botfinger & Rue de la Bastille ▲ 111

BD BEAUMARCHAIS

R. JEAN-BEAUSIRE

IMP. JEAN-BEAUSIRE

R. DE LA BASTILLE

R. DU PASTEUR-WAGNER

R. AMELOT

BD RICHARD-LENOIR

R. SEDAINE

R. ST-SABIN

R. DAVAL

R. DE LA ROQUETTE

COUR. DU CANTAL

PASS. DU CHEVAL-BLANC

R. DU FAUBOURG-ST-ANTOINE

R. DE CHARENTON

R. DE LYON

PL. DE LA BASTILLE

Bastille

BD. BOURDON

BD DE LA BASTILLE

PARIS ARSENAL

① ② ③ ④ ⑤ ⑥ ⑦ ⑧ ⑨ ⑩ ⑪ ⑫ ⑬ ⑭ ⑯

Bastille

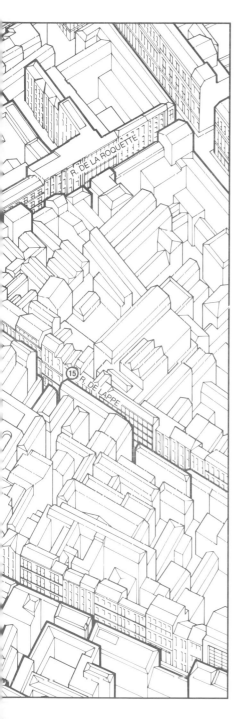

(1) The **rue des Tournelles** (*see page 111*), originally ran beside the royal Palais des Tournelles, demolished by Catherine de Médicis after Henri II's accidental death there in a tournament in 1559. (2) At No. 38, **L'Oulette** (**FF**), a tiny bistrot specializing in tasty dishes from the south-west (*see page 111*). (3) Ninon de Lenclos, the 17thC *femme de lettres* (and mistress of many a great man) who left Voltaire 2000 *livres* in her will to buy books, lived at **No. 36** (*see page 111*). (4) The **Hôtel de Mansart Saganne**, behind No. 28 (best seen from 23 boulevard Beaumarchais), built for his own use by Jules Hardouin-Mansart, the architect of the place Vendôme and the place des Victoires, the dome of Les Invalides and the Grand Trianon at Versailles. (5) **Statue of Beaumarchais**, cane tucked under his arm; he lived in a grand mansion nearby, on the site of Nos 2-20 in his eponymous boulevard (*see page 111*). (6) **Bofinger** (5 rue de la Bastille, **FFF**), fashionable brasserie with riotous art nouveau décor. In the same street, (7) **Le Coin du Caviar** (No. 2, **FF-FFF**), for a luxury snack or a full-scale meal. (8) When his family left Paris, Balzac lived in an attic at **9 rue de Lesdiguières** (*see page 125*), described in *La Peau de Chagrin* as having 'grimy, yellowing walls, with the stench of poverty about it'. Marked out on the paving of (9) the **place de la Bastille**, the outline of the notorious fortress prison whose storming on 14 July 1789 signalled the start of the French Revolution. The bold design of (10) the **Opéra de la Bastille** (Bastille Opera House), opened to celebrate the bicentenary of that momentous event, is by Carlos Ott, a Uruguyan architect living in Canada. (11) But the lofty **Colonne de Juillet** (July Column), topped by a gilded 'Genius of Liberty' perched precariously on one foot, commemorates the victims of a later uprising, the July Revolution of 1830, that put Louis-Philippe on the throne. (12) The **Bassin de l'Arsenal**, chic marina from which boats ply along the Canal Saint-Martin to the Parc de la Villette (*see pages 28-9*). (13) The busy **rue de la Roquette**, worth exploring for its picturesque old houses, its covered arcades and its increasingly trendy bars. (14) At No. 13, **L'Ecluse Bastille**, one of a mini-chain of chic wine bars. (15) The boutiques and art galleries spawned by the arrival of the glitterati in this up-and-coming area exist cheek by jowl with the plebeian bars in the **rue de Lappe**, where the famous turn-of-the-century dance hall Balajo is still in business (No. 9). (16) The **rue du Faubourg-St-Antoine** has been lined with furniture workshops for centuries.

SQ. BOUCICAUT

Sèvres Babylone

BD RASPAIL

PL. ALPHONSE-
DEVILLE

R. DU CHERCHE MIDI

R. COËTLOGON

R. DE RENNES

R. D'ASSAS

R. DE SÈVRES

Rennes

▲ 100

Sèvres-Babylone

▲ 101

▶ 116

(1) The **rue de Sèvres** is well known for its fun fashion boutiques like Tiffany's (No. 12) and for chic-er places like (2) **Marie-Martine** (No. 8). (3) Chic is the keynote of the old-established **Hôtel Lutétitia-Concorde** (**FFF**, with value-for-money brasserie), now that it has been refurbished in extravagant art déco style by *couturière* Sonia Rykiel, whose ready-to-wear boutique is at (4) **4-8 rue de Grenelle**. (5) The **square Boucicaut** (children's playground) commemorates the philanthropist Aristide Boucicaut, who founded the city's first department store, (6) **Les Magasins du Bon Marché** (off map) and ran it with his energetic wife Marguerite. (7) Madame Récamier did not hold her celebrated *salon* in (8) the **rue Récamier**, with, at the end, (9) the **Théâtre Récamier**, once the home of the magical Renaud-Barrault company, but in one wing of a former abbey in (10) the **rue de la Chaise**. Here she lived for thirty years, from the age of forty-two, receiving her platonic admirer Chateaubriand every afternoon at 3 o'clock precisely, followed by all the literary lions of the age. (11) **No. 7** in this old street, a mansion dating from 1763, was briefly owned in the early 19thC by Napoleon's big sister Elisa, Princess Bacchiochi, who sold it to the emperor in 1807. (12) **Au Sauvignon** (80 rue des Saints-Pères), fashionable (and expensive) wine bar. (13) The **carrefour de la Croix-Rouge** once centred on a huge red crucifix (hence the name). Its chief adornment today is (14) a **statue of a centaur** by the *enfant terrible* of modern sculpture, César: his homage to another *enfant terrible*, Picasso. (15) Jacques Copeau's influential productions at the **Théâtre du Vieux-Colombier** (No. 21 in the street of the same name) starred actors of the calibre of Louis Jouvet and Charles Dullin. (16) Some rooms in the charming **Hôtel Abbaye St-Germain** (10 rue Cassette, **FFF**) have their own balconies. (17) The well-bred young foreigners who learn French at the **Institut Catholique** like to refer to it as the 'Catho'. (18) The **rue du Cherche-Midi** is a happy hunting ground for gourmets, with several well-known restaurants: **Joséphine** (No. 117, **FFF**), popular with a media crowd; **Le Gourmet gourmand** (No. 72, **FF-FFF**); and **La Marlotte** (No. 55, **FFF**), a favourite with publishers.

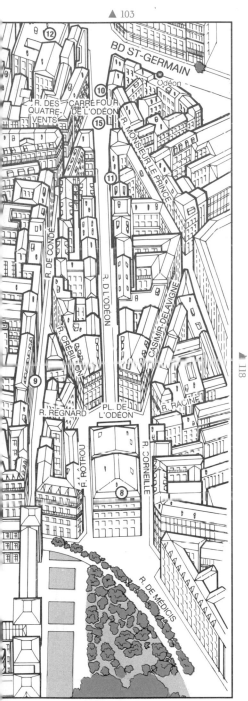

Saint-Sulpice

① For two or three days towards the end of June, the large **place St-Sulpice** plays host to a lively Poetry Market. Poetry publishers display their wares in marquees grouped round ② the **Fontaine des Quatre Evêques** (Four Bishops Fountain), an imposing structure adorned with lions and with statues of four of France's great bishop-orators, Bossuet, Fénélon, Fléchier and Massillon. ③ The **church of Saint-Sulpice**, originally a medieval parish church attached to the abbey of St-Germain-des-Prés (*see page 103*), was rebuilt and enlarged many times over the centuries and is now mainly classical, with an imposing colonnaded west front topped by a pair of towers of unequal height. ④ **Saint-Laurent Rive Gauche**, one of many chic ready-to-wear fashion boutiques run by top designers in this area. ⑤ **Castel** (15 rue Princesse), a private nightclub notoriously hard to get into. ⑥ The **Palais du Luxembourg** (entrance 15 rue de Vaugirard), built by Salomon de Brosse for Henri IV's widow Marie de Médicis, on the lines of the Pitti Palace in her native Florence; the libary, decorated by Delacroix, can usually be visited on Sundays. ⑦ The **Petit Luxembourg** stages occasional art exhibitions. ⑧ The **Théâtre National de l'Odéon**, built in 1782 for the Comédie française troupe of actors, now often puts on foreign companies visiting France. One notable first performance at this theatre was that of *The Marriage of Figaro* by Beaumarchais, who lived nearby at ⑨ **26 rue de Condé**, now a publishing stronghold. ⑩ The deluxe **Relais St-Germain** (**FFF**, 9 carrefour de l'Odéon) and ⑪ the **Odéon** (**FF-FFF**, 3 rue de l'Odéon) are just two of the many small *hôtels de charme* near the Luxembourg Gardens. ⑫ The stylish shoes at **Flash** (115 boulevard St-Germain) are so comfortable that the shop has loyal customers all over France. ⑬ The **Marché St-Germain**, a covered market combined with a swimming-pool and other amenities. ⑭ The **Librairie des Femmes** (74 rue de Seine, off map), a lively and stylish feminist bookshop. ⑮ a **statue of Danton** in the carrefour de l'Odéon, a busy crossroads, stands on the very spot where he once lived. ⑯ **La Petite Cour** (**FF-FFF**, 8 rue Mabillon), really does have a little courtyard-terrace for cool and peaceful summer dining, while at No. 10, ⑰ **Aux Charpentiers** (**FF**) is famous as the one-time headquarters of the Carpenters' Guild.

R. DE L'ÉPERON

R. DANTON

R. MIGNON

R. SERPENTE

R. HAUTEFEUILLE

BD ST-MICHEL

R. DE LA HARPE

R. DE L'ÉCOLE-DE-MÉDECINE

R. HAUTEFEUILLE

R. PIERRE-SARRAZIN

Cluny la Sorbonne

BD ST-GERMAIN

R. RACINE

R. MONSIEUR LE PRINCE

PL. PAUL PAINLEVÉ

BD ST-MICHEL

R. CHAMPOLLION

R. DE LA SORBONNE

R. DE VAUGIRARD

PL. DE LA SORBONNE

R. VICTOR COUSIN

Odéon/Sorbonne

① The narrow **rue Hautefeuille**, one of the oldest on the Left Bank, houses ② a picturesque 16thC house with a turret, the **Hôtel des Abbés de Fécamp** (No. 5), and ③ **La Lozère** (No. 4, **F**), a little restaurant specializing in rustic dishes from the region of the same name on the edge of the Massif Central. On the other side of ④ the **boulevard St-Germain**, slashed through the district during Baron Haussmann's drastic remodelling of the city (*see page 43*), ⑤ the **rue de l'Ecole-de-Médecine** was the scene in 1793 of the assassination of Marat by Charlotte Corday. ⑥ **Polidor** (41 rue Monsieur-le-Prince, **F**), famous for its low prices, its unchanging repertoire of home-style dishes and its literary past. ⑦ The **Musée de Cluny**, devoted to medieval art, architecture and sculpture, housed in one of Paris's few surviving early medieval domestic buildings; in and outside the museum are some fragments of the Roman baths, also on this site. Just outside the museum's entrance, in the square Paul-Painlevé, are ⑧ a bronze copy of a seated **statue of Montaigne** by Paul Landowski (1875-1961), replacing the marble original, and ⑨ a **monument to Pierre Puvis de Chavannes** (1828-98), whose murals, like some of Landowski's monuments, adorn the Panthéon (*see page 129*). He also painted the mural in the main lecture hall in ⑩ the **Sorbonne**, rebuilt in the 19thC, but founded in the mid-13thC by Louis IX's confessor Robert de Sorbon. Four centuries later, the first rebuilding scheme of what had become the seat of the University of Paris was paid for by Cardinal Richelieu, whose tomb, designed by the royal painter-in-chief Charles Le Brun, is in ⑪ the **Eglise de la Sorbonne**. At the river end of ⑫ the **boulevard St-Michel**, its cafés perpetually thronged with students, is a network of narrow medieval streets, including ⑬ the **rue de la Harpe**, part of the main road leading east out of Roman Lutetia, and the rue St-Séverin, leading to ⑭ the **church of St-Séverin**, famous for its richly carved west front and its double ambulatory centring on a striking twisted column. ⑮ The **Hôtel Collège de France** (7 rue Thénard, **FF**), with some rooms at the top boasting old beams and views of Notre Dame, takes its name from ⑯ one of the Latin Quarter's top teaching establishments, the **Collège de France**, founded by François Ier three centuries after the Sorbonne. ⑰ **Le Balzar** (49 rue des Ecoles, **FF**), old-established brasserie.

► 120

△ ⑧ ⑦

R. ST-JULIEN-LE-PAUVRE

②

⑨

R. GALANDE

③

⑥

①

④

⑩

R. DU FOUARRE

⑤

R. DANTE

R. DES ANGLAIS

PONT AU DOUBLE

R. DE L'HÔTEL

R. DE LA BÛCHERIE

COLBERT

PORT DE MONTEBELLO

JEAN

R. DES GRANDS-DEGRÈS

R. DES TROIS-PORTES

R. FRÉDÉRIC-SAUTON

R. LAGRANGE

R. MAÎTRE-ALBERT

⑮

⑪

⑬

R. DE BIÈVRE

⑭

BD ST-GERMAIN

R. DES BERNADINS

Maubert
Mutualité
Ⓜ

⑫

PL. MAUBERT

⑯

R. DU

R. JEAN-DE-BEAUVAIS

SOMMERARD

R. DES CARMES

R. BASSE-
DES-CARMES

R. MONTAGNE-STE-GENEVIÈVE

⑰

R. DES ÉCOLES

R. MONGE

R. ST-VICTOR

Maubert

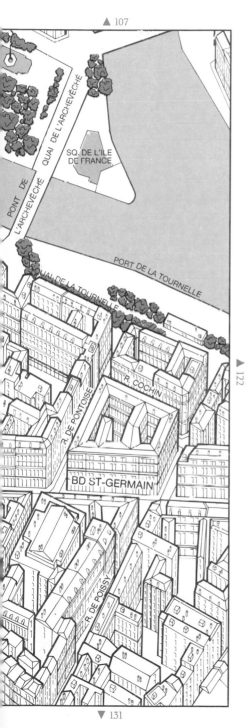

▶ 122

① The oldest tree in Paris, a false acacia planted over three centuries ago, is the pride of the charming **square René-Viviani**, also famous for its lovely close-up views of Notre Dame. Overlooking it, ② the **Hôtel Esméralda** (4 rue St-Julien-le-Pauvre, **FF**), small and popular with showbiz folk. ③ As a backdrop to the square, the Romanesque **church of St-Julien-le-Pauvre**, the site of a 6thC chapel dedicated to one or more St Julians (the experts differ) and attached to a hostel for pilgrims setting out on the road to Santiago de Compostela; since the 1880s its worshippers have been Melchites (a Greek Catholic rite). St Julian the Hospitaller was certainly the church's patron saint at one point. His legend features on a very early carving over the doorway to ④ **No. 42 rue Galande**: a scene depicting the saint and his wife rowing Christ over the river, in the guise of a leper with hooded head. ⑤ The steep medieval gable has survived at **No. 31 rue Galande**. ⑥ **Le Caveau des Oubliettes** (11 rue Galande), a lively cabaret specializing in old French songs. ⑦ **Shakespeare & Co**, a famous bookshop-cum-literary meeting place, has both new and second-hand titles in English. ⑧ **La Bûcherie** (41 rue de la Bûcherie, **FF-FFFF**): cosy open fires in winter, tables outside in summer, delicious newish cuisine and views of Notre Dame year-round. ⑨ **Les Colonies** (10 rue Saint-Julien-le-Pauvre, **FF-FFF**), elegant and charming restaurant right beside the church. ⑩ The **rue du Fouarre** commemorates the bales of straw on which medieval students perched as they listened to open-air lectures by such internationally famous teachers as Albertus Magnus, whose French name appears in ⑪ the **rue Maître-Albert**, one of the picturesque old streets running between the Seine and ⑫ the **place Maubert**, its name probably also derived from a contraction of 'Maître Albert'. ⑬ **Hôtel Notre Dame** (19 rue Maître-Albert, **FF**), well situated for exploring the Latin Quarter and the Île de la Cité and surrounded by lively restaurants, like ⑭ the long-standing **Dodin-Bouffant** (25 rue de Frédéric-Sauton, **FF**) or ⑮ **L'Atelier du Maître-Albert** (1 rue Maître-Albert, **FF**; evenings only) or ⑯ **Diapason** (30 rue des Bernardins, **FF-FFFF**), with elegant décor and a mixture of *nouvelle* and classical cuisine. ⑰ **St-Nicolas-du-Chardonnet**, a bastion of the traditional Latin mass, contains the tomb of the royal painter Charles Le Brun, several of whose paintings adorn the church.

▼ 131

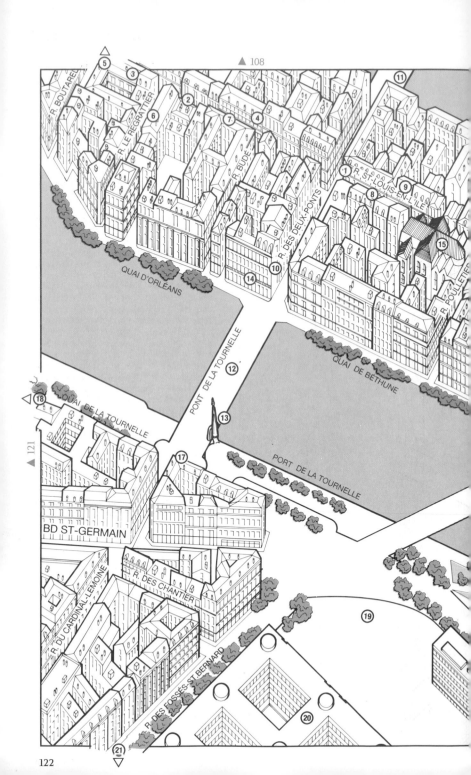

R. BOUTAREL

R. LE REGRATTIER

R. BUDE

R. DES DEUX-PONTS

R. ST-LOUIS-EN-L'ILE

R. POULLETIER

QUAI D'ORLEANS

QUAI DE BETHUNE

PONT DE LA TOURNELLE

QUAI DE LA TOURNELLE

PORT DE LA TOURNELLE

BD ST-GERMAIN

R. DU CARDINAL-LEMOINE

R. DES CHANTIER

R. DES FOSSÉS-ST-BERNARD

Île St-Louis/Tournelles

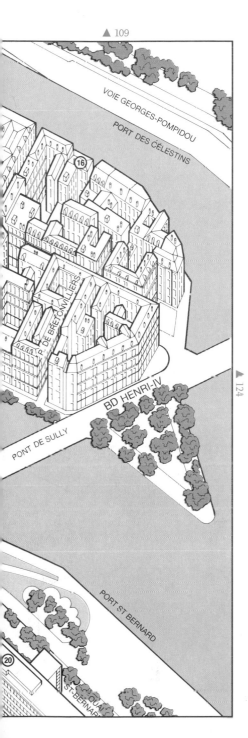

▲ 109

▲ 124

The Île St-Louis's sought-after hotels are all in ① the **rue St-Louis-en-l'Île**, curiously like a busy small town high street with its string of food shops interspersed with restaurants, bookshops and tiny art galleries: ② **Deux-Îles** (No. 59, **FFF**); ③ **Lutèce** (No. 65, **FFF**); ④ **Jeu de Paume** (No. 54, **FFF**), in what was once a 17thC indoor tennis-court (hence the name); and ⑤ **St-Louis** (No. 75, **FF**). ⑥ **Wally Le Saharien** (16/18 rue Le Regrattier, **FFF**), well-known North African restaurant. ⑦ The **Hôtel de Chenizot**, its large balcony supported by griffons, was the home of Thérésa Cabarrus, who was to become famous as 'Our Lady of Thermidor' when she was married to the revolutionary leader Tallien. Aficionados of ice-cream come from far and wide to ⑧ **Berthillon** (35 rue St-Louis-en-l'Île). ⑨ **Au Gourmet de l'Île** (No. 42, **FF**), good-value *cuisine bourgeoise* and lively atmosphere. ⑩ The 18thC novelist and poet Restif de la Bretonne, whose wanderings round Paris at night were recorded in many of his 250-odd books, lived in the **rue des Deux-Ponts**, linking ⑪ the **Pont Marie**, which commemorates the enterprising engineer who developed the island, with ⑫ the **Pont de la Tournelle**, adorned with ⑬ a **statue of Ste Geneviève**, patron saint of Paris. ⑭ **Musée Adam Mickiewicz**, devoted to the Polish poet and patriot who presided over the Polish Library that has been here since 1838. ⑮ **Saint-Louis-en-l'Île**, started by Louis Le Vau, the architect of the Tuileries, parts of the Louvre and Versailles, who himself lived on the island; unusual pierced spire. Among his many lovely mansions, ⑯ the **Hôtel de Lauzun** (open to the public), where Gautier and Baudelaire, both tenants for a while, attended meetings of the Hashish Eaters' Club. ⑰ The **Tour d'Argent** (15-17 quai de la Tournelle, **FFFF**), still one of the world's great restaurants (pressed duck a speciality). A few doors away, ⑱ **La Timonerie** (No. 35, **FF-FFF**), for sunny Mediterranean dishes. ⑲ The stylish eighties **Institut du Monde Arabe** (Arab Institute, with 9th-floor tea-room/restaurant) and ⑳ the earlier and much duller **Science Faculty buildings** (small Museum of Mineralogy in Tour 25) have replaced the Halle aux Vins (wholesale wine market) built by Napoleon to ease pressure on the overcrowded central market (*see page 123*). ㉑ **Moissonnier** (28 rue des Fossés-St-Bernard, **FFF**), long popular for its reliable Lyonnaise cuisine.

R. DES LIONS-SAINT-PAUL

R. DU PETIT-MUSC

R. DE JULES-COUSIN

QUAI DES CÉLESTINS

VOIE GEORGES-POMPIDOU

BD HENRI-IV

SO. H. GALLI

Sully Morland

PONT DE SULLY

R. AGRIPPA-D'AUBIGNÉ

BD MORLAND

QUAI HENRI-IV

R. DE SCHOMBERG

SEINE

▲ 110

▲ 123

▲ 111

① The **rue des Lions-St-Paul** commemorates the royal menagerie built up by Charles V and Charles VI and ② the **quai des Célestins** a large monastery of the Celestine order that once covered most of this Right Bank district. ③ The 16thC **Hôtel Fieubet**, whose interior was redesigned in the 1670s by Jules Hardouin-Mansart for Gaspard de Fieubet, chancellor to Louis XIV's queen, the Infanta Maria Theresa of Spain. It was adorned (or disfigured, depending on your taste) two centuries later with a profusion of motifs borrowed from the Renaissance and the Baroque. ④ **Le Temps des Cerises** (31 rue de la Cerisaie, **F**), one of the few genuinely popular bistrots left in Paris. ⑤ The **Hôtel des Célestins** (**FF**), peaceful small hotel. ⑥ Since 1984 a peculiar sculptural homage to the poet **Arthur Rimbaud** by Ipousteguy has graced the square in front of ⑦ the **Bibliothèque de l'Arsenal**, a specialist theatre library in the only surviving building of a large complex that housed the royal arsenal; the library dates from the mid-18thC (pretty music room). ⑧ The **Pavillon de l'Arsenal**, a tall glass-roofed warehouse converted in 1989 into a lively exhibition centre devoted to town planning in Paris through the ages: an excellent introduction to the history and topography of the city. ⑨ A few chunks of the Bastille Prison (*see pages 112-13*) can be seen in the leafy **square Henri-Galli**, a peaceful spot below which the traffic thunders along ⑩ the **voie Georges-Pompidou**, a much-criticized express road beside the Seine. Plans to create a similar road on the Left Bank were fortunately abandoned. ⑪ The **Pont de Sully**, named after Louis XIV's minister, who lived in the Arsenal, leads to the easternmost tip of the Île St-Louis (*see page 123*) and another peaceful square with ⑫ a **monument to the sculptor Antoine Barye**, who carved the lion on the July Column (*see pages 112-13*). ⑬ The **Hôtel Lambert**, the loveliest and grandest mansion on the island, designed in 1640 by Le Vau and decorated by Le Sueur and Le Brun for wealthy financiers. Voltaire was given shelter here by his 'intimate friend' the beautiful and clever Marquise du Châtelet-Lomont, who translated Newton's *Principia*. ⑭ The gardens below the quai St-Bernard have been turned into the **Musée de la Sculpture en plein air** (Open-air Sculpture Museum, off map), displaying the work of 20thC sculptors. ⑮ The **menagerie** in the Jardin des Plantes (off map, *see location map, page 11*) famously supplied sustenance to the starving populace during the Siege of Paris (1870-71).

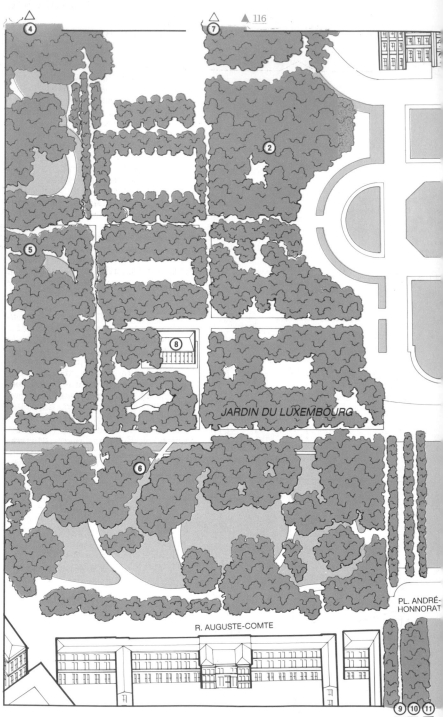

JARDIN DU LUXEMBOURG

PL. ANDRÉ-
HONNORAT

R. AUGUSTE-COMTE

▲ 116

① The southern façade of the **Palais du Luxembourg** forms an elegent backdrop to ② the lovely **Jardin du Luxembourg** (Luxembourg Gardens), dotted with statues and perfect for a romantic stroll, which must include ③ the **Fontaine de Médicis**, a leafy avenue of water leading to the marble figures of the nymph Galatea and her youthful shepherd lover Acis, blissfully ignorant in their transports of love of the menacing bronze Cyclops Polyphemus towering over them in a jealous rage. Among the many statues and monuments, creative artists predominate on the western side of the gardens: ④ a **bust of Beethoven** by Antoine Bourdelle; ⑤ a peculiar **monument to Paul Verlaine** by Rodo de Niederhausen; ⑥ Henri Gauquié's much more appealinig **monument to Antoine Watteau**; and ⑦ a **monument to Eugène Delacroix** by Jules Dalou, in which a series of allegorical figures pay homage to the painter's bust, depicting him at his most withdrawn, even haughty. ⑧ The **Théâtre des Marionnettes** (puppet theatre) has long been attracting crowds of round-eyed children on Wednesday afternoons (half-holiday for schools) and at weekends. At the far end of the gardens, in ⑨ the **allée de l'Observatoire**, is ⑩ a superb fountain, the **Fontaine de l'Observatoire** (off map), the subject of much scathing criticism when it was first erected. Also known as the **Fontaine des Quatre Parties du monde** (Four Parts of the World Fountain), it was the last work of Jean-Baptiste Carpeaux. The idea was to tie in with the presence, at the far end of the avenue, of ⑪ Paris's famous **Observatoire** (Observatory, off map, guided tours first Sat in month, written application required), by devising a fountain symbolically depicting the Planet Earth. Carpeaux's elegant solution was to create a sense of the earth turning on its axis by sculpting four young women, representing Africa, America, Asia and Europe, spinning a globe above their heads, while below them four seahorses by François Rude's nephew Emmanuel Frémiet prance in the spray created by the fountain's jets.

R. CUJAS

R. TOULLIER

R. ST-JACQUES

4 R. SOUFFLOT

9

PL. EDMOND-ROSTAND

5

6

R. LE GOFF

R. MALEBRANCHE

R. PAILLET

Luxembourg (R.E.R.) Ⓜ

7

8

R. DES FOSSÉS-ST-JACQUES

▲ 127

BD. ST MICHEL

IMP. ROYER-COLLARD

R. ROYER-COLLARD

R. GAY LUSSAC

R. PIERRE-ET-MARIE-CURIE

10

11

13

The Panthéon

▲ 119

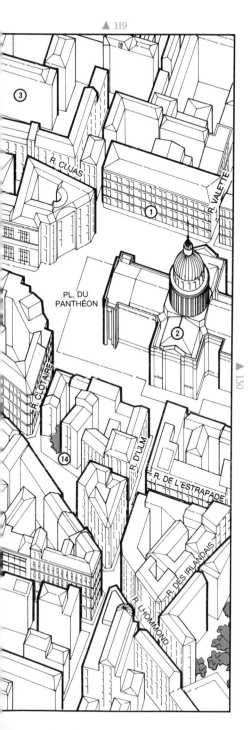

① The library of St Geneviève's abbey (see page 131) forms the nucleus of the collections in the **Bibliothèque Ste-Geneviève** (university library), a nineteenth-century structure with a glass roof on an iron frame, on the site of a famous medieval foundation, the Collège Montaigu. ② The mighty **Panthéon** has had an oddly chequered history: it started life as the fulfilment of a vow by Louis XV that if he recovered from an illness that befell him in Metz he would build a new church to house St Geneviève's tomb. But it changed function several times until it eventually became a national mausoleum to honour illustrious figures like Victor Hugo or Emile Zola. ③ Hugo was a pupil only a few steps away from his last resting place, at the prestigious **Lycée Louis-le-Grand**, where Molière also studied. ④ The **rue Soufflot** commemorates the Panthéon's architect Jean-Germain Soufflot, who died in 1780 before it was completed. On the west side of ⑤ the **place Edmond-Rostand** is one of the entrances to ⑥ the attractive **Jardin du Luxembourg** (Luxembourg Gardens), once the grounds of the palace built for Henri IV's widow, Marie de Médicis. Among the garden's many statues, ⑦ a marble **sculpture of George Sand** by Sicard (1904), clutching a sheaf of manuscript pages and with a somewhat melancholy expression. Nearby, ⑧ a **monument to Stendhal**, with a medallion carved by David d'Angers. The gardens are thronged in term time with undergraduates from the many higher education establishments in and around ⑨ the **rue St-Jacques**, whose name recalls its role as the starting point of a pilgrim route to Santiago de Compostela (St-Jacques de Compostelle in French). Among these institutions are ⑩ the **Institut Océanographique** (Institute of Oceanography), whose 'Centre de la Mer et des Eaux' is open to the public, and ⑪ the **Ecole nationale supérieure de Chimie** (Institute of Chemistry) in ⑫ the **rue Pierre-et-Marie-Curie**, commemorating the joint Nobel prize winners for physics in 1903. ⑬ The 17thC **church of St-Jacques-du-Haut-Pas** (just off map), its portal adorned with Doric columns, was once surrounded by a cemetery, whose inhabitants were transferred to the Catacombs in the 19thC. ⑭ The **Bistrot de la Nouvelle Mairie**, 19 rue des Fossés-St-Jacques, a lively wine bar.

▲ 130

R. DE L'ÉCOLE POLYTECHNIQUE

R. VALETTE

R. MONTAGNE

R. LAPLACE

8

R. ST-ETIENNE-DU-MONT

2

1

R. CLOVIS

5

R. DESCARTES

6

4

R. CLOTHILDE

3

9

10

R. DU CARDINAL-LEMOINE

R. THOUIN

R. DE L'ESTRAPADE

7

R. BLAINVILLE

13

14

R. LAROMIGUIÈRE

R. TOURNEFORT

R. MOUFFETARD

R. ST-MÉDARD

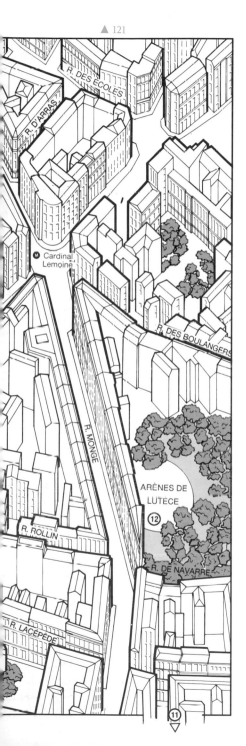

The Montagne Sainte-Geneviève

① A much venerated reliquary containing some fragments of the tomb of Paris's patron saint St Geneviève is the high point of the late Gothic interior of **St-Etienne-du-Mont**, atop the hill named after the one-time shepherdess. ② **Le Vieux Paris (FF)**, a cosy restaurant well endowed with old beams, tucked into a corner site at the top of St Geneviève's hill. ③ A portion of the medieval city wall built by Philippe Auguste can be seen at **3 rue Clovis**. ④ The **rue Clovis** cuts across the site of the Abbaye Ste-Geneviève, a later incarnation of the early 6thC basilica commissioned by the Merovingian King Clovis to house his own tomb and that of his wife Queen Clotilde, as well as the saint's; most of it was destroyed in the French Revolution. ⑤ **La Tour de Clovis** (Clovis's Tower) is a misnomer: with its Romanesque base and Gothic upper storeys it was originally the belfry of the abbey church, built many centuries after Clovis's death in 511. It is now inside the hallowed precincts of ⑥ the **Lycée Henri-IV**, one of the country's top secondary schools, which once had Jean-Paul Sartre on its teaching staff. ⑦ The rue des Irlandais houses the **Collège des Irlandais**, an Irish seminary in an 18thC building now shared with Polish candidates for the priesthood – Karol Wojtyla studied here long before he became the first non-Italian pope for over 450 years. ⑧ The **Jardin de l'École Polytechnique** has kept the name of the most celebrated of France's élite *grandes écoles*, though the college itself was banished to the suburbs after the 'events' of May 1968. ⑨ The **rue du Cardinal-Lemoine** has seen its fair share of celebrities: Pascal died at his sister's house on the site of No. 67 in 1622; James Joyce wrote part of *Ulysses* at No. 71; Ernest Hemingway lived in relative squalor on the third floor of No. 74; and the naturalist Buffon lived in ⑩ the beautiful **Hôtel Le Brun**, built in honour of Louis XIV's 'royal painter-in-chief' Charles Le Brun. Buffon was for nearly half a century keeper of ⑪ the **Jardin des Plantes** (off map), botanical gardens also housing a large natural history museum and a small menagerie. ⑫ The **Arènes de Lutèce** (amphitheatre), a rare survivor of the Roman city of Lutetia. ⑬ Rabelais sang the praises of the Pine Cone Cabaret in the **place de la Contrescarpe**, a tiny square famously described by Hemingway in *The Snows of Kilimanjaro*. ⑭ Running downhill from the square, the **rue Mouffetard**, once the Roman road to Rome (via Lyon), has one of the city's best and oldest food markets.

R. DU CHERCHE-MIDI

R. DE VAUGIRARD

13

VILLA

IMP. DE L'ASTROLABE

IMP. DU MONT-TONNERRE

R. D'ALENÇON

BD DU

GABRIELLE

VILLA GARNIER

5

R. ANTOINE-BOURDELLE

AV. DU MAINE

R. ARMAND MOISANT

Montparnasse-Bienvenüe

1

R. DE L'ARRIVÉE

7

PL. R. DAUTRY

6

BD DE VAUGIRARD

2

AV. DU MAINE

3

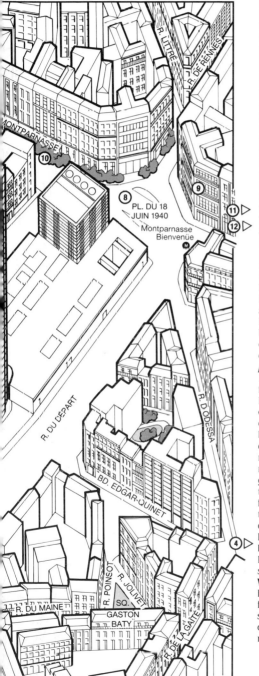

① Since 1973, the fifty-nine-storey **Tour Montparnasse** (extensive views from the top, cafeteria, restaurant) has dominated a once-bohemian district peopled by poets and painters – hence the 'Mount Parnassus' label. ② Near the tower, the **Gare Montparnasse** has been rebuilt to receive trains operating the high-speed service to the Atlantic Coast, launched in 1990. ③ And close to the station, a chance to see the work of Spanish architect Ricardo Bofill in the **place de Catalogne** (off map): two six-storey blocks called 'L'Amphithéâtre' and 'Les Colonnes'. ④ The **Cimetière du Montparnasse** (also off map) houses the tombs of many an artist and writer, including Jean-Paul Sartre and Simone de Beauvoir, and the Russian sculptor Ossip Zadkine, whose home and studio can be visited not far away, at 100bis rue d'Assas. ⑤ The **Musée Bourdelle** displays the work of another sculptor, Antoine Bourdelle (1860-1929), whose work includes the romantic monument to the Polish poet Adam Mickiewicz in the cours Albert 1er beside the Seine. (No 16 in the street named after him). ⑥ The **Musée de la Poste and de la Philatélie** (34 boulevard de Vaugirard) is a paradise for stamp collectors and anyone interested in the history of France's postal service. ⑦ The **Maine-Montparnasse Building** at the foot of the tower includes a branch of Paris's chic department store Galeries Lafayette (*see page 47*). ⑧ The busy **place du 18 juin 1940** was so renamed to commemorate the famous call to resistance after the Fall of France, broadcast on that date from London on BBC radio, by an obscure French officer called Charles de Gaulle. ⑨ The large and bustling **Bistro de la Gare** (**F**, 59 boulevard du Montparnasse), one of a chain of restaurants serving value-for-money 'formula' meals, offers the plus of magnificent genuine art nouveau décor. ⑩ East of the tower, the **boulevard du Montparnasse** is famous for its long-standing brasseries, once the haunt of local writers and artists, especially the American expatriate community. ⑪ **La Coupole** (**FF**, No. 102, off map) and ⑫ **Le Dôme**, now specializing in seafood (**FFFF**, No. 108, also off map), are the best-known survivors of that vanished era. ⑬ The **rue de Vaugirard**, generally said to be the city's longest street, stretches south-westwards as far as the 'boulevards des Marchaux', Parisians' nickname for the ring of boulevards circling the city, all named after famous military men bearing the title Marshal of France.

GENERAL POINTS OF INTEREST

N

O

S

T

T

Tacherie r. de la 106
Talleyrand r. de 80
Tardieu r. 35
Temple r. du 91, 92, 108
Tertre pl. du 33
Thénard r. 119
Thérèse r. 60, 74, 75
Thomy-Thierry allée 78
Thorigny r. de 95
Thouin r. 130
Tilsitt r. de 37
Tiquetonne r. 77
Tiron r. 108
Toullier r. 128
Tour-Maubourg bd. de la 67
Tour-Saint-Jacques sq. de la 90
Tournefort r. 130
Tournelle pont de la 121, 122, 123
Tournelle quai de la 121, 122, 123
Tournelles r. des 111, 112, 113
Tournon r. de 116
Tourville av. de 96
Toustain r. 116
Traktir r. de 36
Trémoille r. de la 51
Trésor r. du 108-9
Trocadéro-et-du-11-Novembre pl. du 64, 65
Trois-Frres r. des 34-5
Trois-Portes r. des 120
Tronchet r. 45, 46, 47
Tronson-du-Coudray r. 44
Trudaine av. 35
Tuileries port des 70-1, 84
Tuileries quai des 70-1, 84-5
Turbigo r. de 77
Turenne r. de 94, 95, 110

U

Ulm r. d' 129
Université r. de l' 79, 80-1, 81, 82-3, 84, 85, 100-1, 101
Ursins r. des 106
Uzes r. d' 62-3

V

Valette r. 129, 130
Valois galerie de 74-5
Valois pl. de 75
Valois r. de 75
Vaneau cité 97
Vaneau r. 98
Varenne cité de 98
Varenne r. de 96-7, 97, 98-9, 99
Varsovie pl. de 65
Vauban pl. 96, 97
Vaugirard bd. de 132
Vaugirard r. de 115, 116, 117, 118, 132, 133
Vauvilliers r. 88
Velasquez av. 41
Vendôme pl. 58, 59, 113
Venise r. de 90
Ventadour r. de 60
Vernet r. 37
Verneuil r. de 84-5, 85
Véron r. 34
Verrerie r. de la 91, 92, 108
Vert-Galant sq. du 89
Viarmes r. de 76
Victoire r. de la 47
Victoires pl. des 76, 77, 113
Victor-Cousin r. 118, 128
Victor-Hugo av. 36
Victoria av. 89, 90, 106
Vieille-du-Temple r. 92-3, 94, 95, 108
Vieuville r. de la 34
Vieux-Colombier r. du 114-15, 115
Vignon r. 46, 47, 58
Villars av. de 96
Ville-l'Evêque r. de la 44
Villehardouin r. 95
Villersexel r. de 82-3
Visconti r. 102
Viollet-le-Duc r. 34
Villedo r. 74
Vivienne r. 61, 62, 63
Volney r. 58
Volta r. 93
Voltaire quai 85
Vosges pl. des 110-11, 111